D1604480

Emergency Food
in a
Nutshell

Leslie D. Probert and Lisa L. Harkness

Purely Simple Publishing, LLC

Contents

ACKNOWLEDGMENTS

We would like to acknowledge and thank the members of our monthly "Neighborhood Food Storage Group." At our monthly meetings, these neighbors and friends shared information on food storage sales and sources and on food preparation and preserving techniques. Together we placed group orders and shared recipes as we experimented with our own food storage supplies. We thank the following inventive women for freely sharing their ideas and opinions:

Renae Allen   Marguerite Madsen
Tatiana Allen   Darla McCoy
Elaine Augustine   Sylvia Morales
Carolyn Bargeron   Kathy Muirhead
Julie Beckstrand   Charlotte Putman
Anna Benally   Laurel Rapp
Julie Burns   Marianna Robins
Lisa Joner   Shannon Slinker

We have delighted in the enthusiasm and encouragement this group has mutually given its members and appreciate the collective dedication these women demonstrate as they store food for themselves and their families. Belonging to this group has been sure proof that acquiring food storage can be fun!

Special thanks to Tresa Hansen and Patrice Hansen for their insight and recipes given during monthly food storage luncheons—and to other extended family members who have also submitted great recipes.

We appreciate close friends who have been kind enough to preview various parts of this book and provide us with a fresh perspective. We especially thank Judy Harris of the Utah State University Extension Service, who has graciously given of her time to help us find answers to our hard questions, and who has freely shared her resources.

We are indebted to the following professionals who have generously shared their knowledge and expertise: Ken Bousfield and Eva Nemanski, Utah Department of Environmental Quality; Gerard Yates, Central Utah Water Conservancy District; Ed Jackson, Brigham Young University; Oscar Pike, Brigham Young University; Baron Glassgow, National Propane Gas Association; Dr. Harold Smith, National Kerosene Heater Association; Doug Hyer, Jardine Petroleum Company; Richard Sparwasser, Omni Environmental Services; Jack Stauffenberg, Blaschak Coal Company.

We especially thank Kim Butler, Jana Erickson, Dave Harkness, and Randall Pixton for going out of their way to help us with the artwork and technical layout of this book.

And finally, we thank our dear families who have patiently devoted their taste buds to our food storage recipe experiments (they've eaten many icky recipes to help us find the delicious ones). Our love for them is our greatest motivation.

We are continuing to learn about storing food. This book represents the best information we have found so far.

INTRODUCTION
SAVING ACORNS FOR WINTER

"Once upon a time there was a little fat comfortable grey squirrel, called Timmy Tiptoes. He had a nest thatched with leaves in the top of a tall tree; and he had a little squirrel wife called Goody.

"Timmy Tiptoes sat out, enjoying the breeze; he whisked his tail and chuckled—'Little wife Goody, the nuts are ripe; we must lay up a store for winter and spring.'

"Goody Tiptoes was busy pushing moss under the thatch—'The nest is so snug, we shall be sound asleep all winter.' 'Then we shall wake up all the thinner, when there is nothing to eat in spring-time,' replied prudent Timothy.

"When Timmy and Goody Tiptoes came to the nut thicket, they found other squirrels were there already.

"Timmy took off his jacket and hung it on a twig; they worked away quietly by themselves.

"Everyday they made several journeys and picked quantities of nuts. They carried them away in bags, and stored them in several hollow stumps near the tree where they had built their nest." (Beatrix Potter, The Tale of Timmy Tiptoes, pg. 9-14.)

Just like the fictional squirrels in this tale by Beatrix Potter, any child can tell you that real squirrels do indeed store acorns for winter. It is interesting to note that while some squirrels hibernate and survive on their caches in sparse springtime, many do not hibernate and need a large supply of nuts and seeds for both winter and spring. There are even squirrels in Africa that store seeds as a provision against the hot season when the trees have generally no seed. All squirrels gather instinctively, not knowing beforehand whether the anticipated lean season will be short or long, severe or mild. They collect what the pouches of their mouths can hold, nimbly scurrying from source to cache until there is a sufficient supply. Their gleaning proceeds in a focused, deliberate manner even as they continue to take care of their current appetites.

There is much we can learn from squirrels. They are prepared in all seasons and for all circumstances. Knowing their physical limitations, they gather what they can. And their ultimate success in obtaining their goal lies in their persistent and steady efforts. All of us will encounter lean seasons at some time in our lives. When we do, will we, like squirrels, have enough to sustain ourselves and those we love? Our own instinctive sense of self-preservation coupled with love for our families bids us to establish a storage of food.

The term "food storage" in this book refers to that supply of food set aside for any time of limited resources. People in every corner of the globe have historically stored food in anticipation of leaner times. In recent decades, ecclesiastical leaders of the Church of Jesus

Christ of Latter-day Saints have been counseling their members to store at least a year's supply of food and other necessities. Other churches as well, have offered similar counsel. Storing food helps us prepare for our own "winters" or "sparse springs."

Before the time when we, the authors, became neighbors, we had each been interested in and followed current events. As we did so, we were troubled by the effects of particular natural and manmade disasters. We noticed how the subsequent emergencies posed by these crises often left people without food or water to drink. Both of us wondered how we would react in such emergencies, and immediately our thoughts turned to our children and families. We both feared hearing the hungry cries of our children and could imagine ourselves feeling guilty for not preparing to feed them in an emergency. Understanding our responsibility, we each set out to establish our own food storage.

Our initial attempts to store food raised difficult questions. We put our minds together, dug in our heels, and refused to give up until we found the answers we were looking for. Our quest for reliable information has been a three-year adventure, and we're excited to be able to share it with you!

Our goal has been to keep food storage simple, inexpensive, space efficient, and delicious with an emphasis on nutrition. This book is unique in that it takes a person from the earliest planning stages to cooking with 100% food storage ingredients. We have also taken great care to make sure recipes are fuel efficient and have included a well- researched appendix on fuel storage and cooking options. Recipes included in this book use powdered eggs and butter because, in an emergency, most of us will not have access to fresh ingredients. You'll be amazed at how easy it is to bake in the inexpensive applebox reflector oven described in this book!

Our inspiration in this project was born of our profound knowledge that God has a prophet on the earth through whom he has given counsel to store a year's supply. This gave us the confidence that if we kept trying we would surely find the solutions we needed. We acknowledge His hand in helping us find answers to our questions and joy in reaching our goals. We can personally attest to the tangible feeling of peace that comes from being prepared. It is our sincere hope that you, too, will feel this peace as you "gather your acorns."

"YES, BUT . . . ."
COMMON OBSTACLES AND PRACTICAL SOLUTIONS

Why would I want to store food?

Before the conveniences of modern technology, people used to store food in root cellars to prepare for the coming winter. This stored food supplied families with fresh food after the growing season was over. In our society today, we don't use such cellars because we can buy food year round at a grocery store. Yet, if you look in your own cupboards or fridge, you will probably find an extra package of pasta or a few extra cans of vegetables. Without realizing it, you have already begun to store food. Why are you doing this? So you will have food on hand, be it for tomorrow's dinner or next week's lunch. Basically, you store food so that it will be there when you need it.

In recent decades, government agencies and ecclesiastical leaders have encouraged emergency preparedness. This emergency preparedness includes having enough food on hand for your needs.

Isn't having a store of food an outdated precaution?

While it is true that the encouragement to store food for times of emergency is not new, it cannot be considered outdated. After all, as long as you have a body, you need food. Additionally, as long as life's experiences are unpredictable, there is a need to prepare for times of want and need.

You may have heard of people storing food for some eventual emergency and then never needing it because the emergency never materialized. Some worry about wasting time or energy in pursuit of such storage if they will never use it. Why not think of storing food as a type of "calorie" insurance? You buy fire insurance or earthquake insurance for the possibility of such a calamity. And yet at the same time, you hope that you will never have to make a claim on your policy. It would be wonderful if life never presented us with a situation in which we needed to rely upon the food stored in our homes. But what if it does? Would we have "calorie" insurance? Food storage can provide us with peace of mind; knowing that in the event of an emergency we would still have food to eat.

When would I find my food storage valuable?

Your food storage will be valuable in a variety of situations. Some of these could last for a long period of time while others may last only a couple of months. Consider the following events: abnormal weather patterns (extreme temperatures, floods or droughts), natural disasters, regional crop failures or infestations, loss or change in employment, decrease in wages, extended illness or permanent disability, transportation or other labor strikes, world economic fluctuations, national turmoil (war), or even increasing inflation and high food prices.

As you can see, though we live in a relatively wealthy and technologically advanced society, we are still susceptible to many of the difficulties experienced by man throughout history. Our modern society actually presents us with vulnerabilities unknown to past generations. Common sense tells us that we need to be wisely prepared. Whatever the situation, your food storage will not only help you survive, but also provide you with a sense of stability and comfort in a trying time.

In a crisis, why can't I just rely on community, government, or extended family resources for help?

Naturally in many, if not in all of the situations listed above, community and government resources and assistance would be stretched to their limits. If a particular crisis were to continue for months at a time, emergency provisions would dwindle quickly. Therefore, it would not be wise to rely solely upon such assistance.

If you are planning to turn to your extended family for assistance, have you spoken to them and made a plan with them? Otherwise, it is important to make a plan for you and your own family.

How many months' supply should I have on hand?

Many people do not have more than a week's supply of food in their homes. And while a week's supply is better than none in a crisis, better still would be a few month's supply. However, considering the varied situations which could realistically cause us to rely solely upon the food we have in our own homes, some organizations and churches are recommending that we store *at least a year's supply of food*. Many crises do not go away in a month or two and some may even take up to a year or longer to resolve. Certainly, having a year's supply of food will help us be prepared for most difficulties.

In my busy schedule, how can I find time to plan for or acquire my food storage?

While it is true that this will take time, it doesn't have to be accomplished in one week or even one year. Planning what you will store and how much to store can seem overwhelming. The section, "Making Your Plan," very simply lays out food options and storage quantities for quick and efficient planning.

Thereafter, acquiring the food on your plan is made easier by concentrating on only a few items each month. The section entitled "Gathering Calender: A Yearly Purchasing Plan" will help you conserve both time and energy by organizing monthly purchases according to seasonal sales and harvest cycles.

How can I afford the expense of acquiring my food storage?

This may be the most daunting challenge for most people. Certainly, acquiring a year's supply of food will cost more than the weekly grocery bill. This concern has been foremost in our minds as we gathered and put together all our information on food storage. Our entire approach to food storage has been to make food storage as cost efficient as possible.

Your commitment to being prepared and desire for peace of mind will help you stretch a tight budget. Consider the following ideas. A surprising number of items can be purchased with only a dollar left over from weekly grocery money. This extra grocery

6

money can also be saved to buy an item in larger quantities. You can eat food storage breakfasts instead of expensive boxed cereals and use the savings toward your monthly food storage budget. You can look for seasonal sales on canned or bulk items. You can join/start a co-op, where people work together to buy in bulk, thus reducing the overall price to its members. When there is any discretionary income, like tax returns, you can ask yourself, "Would I rather have _____ or eat when I'm hungry?" You can even ask for or give food storage items for presents on special occasions such as birthdays, anniversaries, bridal showers, or Christmas. Finally, you can ask for divine help through prayer. We can attest that this source, though perhaps frequently overlooked, will be your greatest help in preparing your family.

Making a specific plan, like the one in the next section of this book, gives you focus—when you have a bit of extra money, you know *exactly* where you will spend it. It's also a good idea to set aside a little money from each paycheck for food storage. One note of caution: in your desire to acquire your food storage, you can be tempted to go into debt. Many food storage suppliers offer easy credit when buying their packages. Be careful that your desire for peace of mind isn't undermined by the bondage of financial debt.

How can I convince other members of my family that this should be a priority in our family expenses?

It is important that all members of your family understand what food storage is, why you would want to store food, and what kinds of situations could require you to rely upon it. Involving family members in the plans you make increases commitment.

If you need to prove your point, you could challenge your family to eat only the food currently stored in your fridge or cupboards for an entire week. Once the week is over have your family evaluate the meals they were able to fix. Did they taste good? Where they nutritious? How much food was left over? Would they be able to survive if the experiment were to continue? Most family members will easily understand the need for storing food and will be supportive of carrying out an emergency food storage plan.

What do I really need to store?

To survive, you need only acquire a few basic items: grains, dried legumes, sugar or honey, milk, fat or oil, salt, and water. Besides helping us survive, these foods have many advantages. They are the *least expensive, are highly nutritious, take less space to store, and most store for a very long time.* Whole grains and beans form a complete protein, making them a meat substitute.

Aren't these foods boring and tasteless?

By themselves, yes, they are. A good example of this is found in the recollections of pioneer John Young as he recorded, "how poor and same-like" his family's diet of corn bread, salt bacon, and a little milk seemed. He said that mush and bacon became so nauseating that eating it was like taking medicine and he had difficulty swallowing it (as quoted in <u>Our Heritage</u>, 1996, pg. 72). Expanding your food storage to include more than the seven basics gives you and your family both the additional nutrition and variety needed to maintain healthy appetites. Food that is appealing is also a vital psychological comfort in a crisis situation.

Having a variety of meals is also critical. Who among us would be excited about eating the same five soup recipes week after week? A pool of varied recipes makes meals appealing. Menus can be kept interesting by storing and using canned meats in place of beans. Because of the importance of variety, we have included two months of main dish recipes using beans and canned meats.

All the recipes in this book have been put together with taste, variety, and nutrition as priorities. They use the seven basic survival foods as well as canned and dried foods in a variety of delicious ways. Appendix B will show you how to convert some of your family favorite recipes into ones using food storage ingredients without a significant sacrifice in taste. Deciding what recipes you'll fix, either from this book or from your own family favorites, makes it easy to create a list of expanded food storage items you'll need. In the section "Making Your Expanded Food Storage Plan", you will find an easy place to record the additional ingredients, other than the basics, that your recipes require.

Can I get enough nutrition from dried or canned foods?

Yes. The key is to store a variety of foods which, in their nutrients, compensate for each other. While one food will be low in some nutrients, another food will be high in those nutrients and low in others. The important thing is to be sure to include fruits and vegetables that are as high as possible in vitamin A and particularly vitamin C, which is easily destroyed.

Dried and canned foods are exposed to high temperatures which decrease vitamin levels. However, both still make a nutritional contribution to any diet. In analyzing a two-day menu based on the Food Pyramid using milk, grains, and only canned foods, it was possible to meet the RDI for every major nutrient except iron, which was met with the addition of a little bit of dried fruit to the diet. Dried and canned foods will be invaluable in seasons of the year when garden vegetables and fruits cannot be grown.

The University of California, Berkeley says, "Fresh veggies and fruits [purchased in a grocery store] are not always the most nutritious, since many are harvested before they're ripe, trucked thousands of miles, and stored for long periods—in which case nutrient loses can be substantial. Thanks to improved technology, canned foods retain most of the food's vitamins and minerals. The heating process of commercial canning partly destroys some vitamins, but some nutrient loss is inevitable whenever food is prepared."

Where do I go to buy the food I will store?

Besides your local grocery store, there are various places that sell foods packaged for long-term storage. You may want to start in the phone book looking under the topics Food Products, Food Storage, Food—Dehydrated & Freeze Dried, or Grocers—Wholesale.

Some companies also offer one year food storage units containing a variety of foods. These can be convenient, but costly, and may not always meet personal taste preferences.

Other good resources include mail order suppliers that provide a wide variety of food storage items. Request catalogs to review their range of products. To get you started, we have included a small list of reliable suppliers, from the Intermountain West, in Appendix H. Check the Internet for others that service your area.

What kind of packaging should I look for when I buy my food storage?

Most importantly, look for food *packaged* for long-term storage: containers that are opaque, airtight/moisture proof, and have oxygen depleted environments. This prolongs nutrition, shelf life, and prevents insect infestation. Opaque containers prevent light from entering and destroying vitamins. Airtight/moisture proof containers keep both air and moisture away from the food which can cause it to deteriorate more rapidly. An oxygen depleted environment is one in which the oxygen has been removed with either an oxygen absorber packet or by some other method. In the absence of oxygen, food will last longer and any insect eggs cannot survive.

Of course, canned items purchased from grocery stores meet these requirements. Other examples of this type of packaging include #10 cans, mylar bags (often packed inside 5 or 6 gallon plastic buckets), and airtight, 5-6 gallon plastic buckets. Keep in mind that larger containers are heavy to lift, move, and stack. However, #10 cans come six to a box and are easy to carry and very space efficient to stack.

Buying food in bulk quantities not packaged for long-term storage can be a saving. But understand that you will need to use these large packages within a reasonable time to ensure the quality of the food.

Where and how should I store a year's supply of food?

The optimum storage space would be one that is cool (about 70° F), dark (in a basement), and dry. These three factors: temperature, moisture, and light greatly affect the shelf life of foods, including appearance, taste, and nutrition. Temperature alone greatly affects shelf life: high temperatures will significantly decrease shelf life, while low temperatures will maintain or possibly extend it. Humidity or moisture in the air will affect metal containers, causing them to rust and corrode. Light not only increases temperature, but can destroy vitamin content if it penetrates the container at all.

While storing food in a basement is the ideal, many residences do not have such a resource. Many condominiums and apartments have limited storage space. In these cases, you have to do the best you can while considering the above factors. With a little creativity, you can find more space than you think. For example, a closet can be used or reorganized to accommodate an amazing amount of food. You can store boxes or plastic buckets under your bed, even substituting them for the bed frame. Surprisingly, three hundred pounds of wheat, stored in #10 cans, can be attractively covered with a cloth and used as a side or end table. The bottom line is, if you want your food storage, you will find a place to put it. Refer to Appendix A for details on these and other storage space ideas. It is important to remember that because *severe* heat alters the appearance, taste, and vitamin content of foods, places such as sheds, garages, or rented storage spaces are undesirable.

Food stored in metal containers (cans, barrels) should be kept off cement floors. Place them on wooden blocks or pallets to prevent condensation and rust. Additionally, allow for air space between containers, floor, and walls to reduce chances of condensation.

I'm afraid that all this food storage will be too bulky. What do I do with it when I have to move?

If it is too difficult to take it with you, there are still other options. For example, if you've kept your food storage in good condition, you can sell it to an interested family. This money can then be used to buy new supplies when you settle in your new area. If you know about your move well enough in advance, you can use all or part of your food storage before moving. This would eliminate or at least decrease the amount you have to move and also save money on groceries. Again, this saved money can be used to replenish supplies. If you're not able to do any of these things, you can always give it away to family members, friends, or neighbors. Many organizations that serve the needy would also be interested in such donations.

How long will my stored food will last?

Most foods have a "Best if Used By" date. This is usually a conservative estimate that takes into account the varied conditions under which that item might be stored. As we have mentioned, storage conditions and packaging greatly influence the shelf life of food. When properly stored and packaged, shelf life estimates are reliable. Even though packaged properly, less than optimum storage conditions can decrease shelf life, and it is hard to say with exactness how long a particular food item will last.

After contacting a number of sources, including food manufacturers and distributors, we have compiled some general shelf life guidelines found in the section entitled "How Long Will These Acorns Last Anyway?: Basic and Expanded Shelf Life Information."

How do I use my food storage before the shelf life expires?

Because food won't retain its optimum nutrition and taste forever, you will need to use your stored food items regularly. This is called rotating, which means consuming your food storage before its optimum nutrition and taste have expired. Rotating helps you use your food storage before it develops off-flavors and the nutritional value seriously diminishes. It also encourages you to learn how to prepare your food in delicious ways. Then, in an emergency, you will already know what to cook, eliminating the stress of having to figure it out.

Some people find it hard to break open food purchased in large buckets because of their expense. Somehow it's easier to open and use food from a smaller #10 can than from a whole bucket. If this applies to you, consider buying your food in smaller containers.

Experience has taught us to keep at least a small container of *every* food storage item in our kitchens. This way we are reminded to use everything we store regularly. Large containers kept in a basement can be rotated in this way. Buying food in #10 cans, which fit in a kitchen pantry or cupboard, keeps rotating simple.

I'm a busy person and don't have time to cook wheat and beans. Since wheat and beans have a long shelf life, can't I just leave them stored until I need them?

While wheat does last a very long time, beans have a shorter shelf life of 8 years. The older the bean the longer it will take to soften. Very old beans will not soften even if you cook them all day!

You will want to regularly include these high fiber foods in your diet now. A sudden increase in fiber will upset the digestive system. That's why its critical, if you're storing these foods, to start eating them now. The health benefits are enormous and your body will already be used to eating them in an emergency.

Some people are concerned about gas from eating beans. There are simple ways to alleviate this concern. First, draining the soaking and cooking water from beans minimizes gas. Secondly, storing canned beans and draining them before adding to a recipe also reduces gas. Canned beans are the gentlest to sensitive digestive systems. Finally, according to Oregon State University, eating beans regularly is the best way to overcome problems with gas. After a while people just get used to them.

Time has been a major consideration in the development of all our recipes. While all of us are very busy today, in an emergency time and energy will need to be conserved. All our recipes are designed to use a minimum amount of time to prepare and cook. You will find our fast bread and quick mix recipes easy to use. Of course, a bread maker is a quick option when making whole-wheat bread. You will also enjoy our ideas for amazingly fast bean preparation (see Appendix B). All of our bean recipes can be prepared with time saving canned beans, if desired.

How can I convince members of my family to eat meals cooked with our food storage?

Enlisting your family support in deciding what food to store is essential. For example, let them sample several brands of milk and decide together which one to store. Prepare food storage recipes and let them choose which ones they would like to eat. Soliciting their input will make rotating easier.

Having a pool of recipes that your family enjoys is critical to keeping food storage meals interesting. This book contains a variety of family-tested, 100% food storage recipes for you to try. They cover a wide range of tastes, including familiar, classic, and unusual recipes. There are meat and meatless recipes, time-saving mixes, fast bread and tortilla recipes, and morale boosting desserts and treats.

Fixing food storage meals two days a week allows you to rotate an entire year's supply of food within the shelf life of most foods (3½ years). This enables you to enjoy your usual fresh and favorite foods while at the same time experiencing several significant benefits. For example, stored foods are consumed quickly, eliminating the need of tracking numerous shelf life dates. You will also know how to cook with food storage items, and your family will be used to eating the recipes you prepare. And finally, your body will be used to the healthy, high-fiber foods you have stored.

I'm excited about acquiring my food storage, but I'm aware that my neighbors have none. What will I do in a crisis situation when they need food?

This is indeed a perplexing question. Before a crisis comes, it's a good idea to try to get your friends and neighbors interested in acquiring food storage. You may also want to share with them some of the recipes you make with your stored food.

However, when a crisis arrives and your neighbors are still without food, the following counsel from Vaughn J. Featherstone may be helpful.

"'Do we have to share with them?' No, we don't *have* to share — we *get* to share! Let us not be concerned about silly thoughts of whether we would share or not. Of course we would share! What would Jesus do? I could not possibly eat food and see my neighbors starving. And if you starve to death after sharing, 'greater love hath no man than this...' (John 15:13.)

"Now what about those who would plunder and break in and take that which we have stored for our family's needs? Don't give this one more idle thought. There is a God in Heaven...He said, 'If ye are prepared, ye need not fear.'" (Doctrine & Covenants 38:30; *Ensign*, Nov. 1976, pg. 117-18.)

Where do I start? There seems to be so much to do!

Let us remind you of these three simple steps. First, make your plan by figuring out just how much of which foods you want to store. Second, evaluate your budget and priorities to find ways to purchase the food in your plan. And third, follow your plan by doing a little every month. Discouragement is your enemy. At every step along the way, it is important to constantly focus on what you *are* accomplishing instead of what's left to do. The operative word here is 'Do.' Remember, you don't have to acquire your food storage in one month. ***Even if it takes you several months or a couple of years, you will be able to acquire every item on your plan if you consistently and persistently work at it.***

GETTING STARTED

MAKING YOUR BASIC FOOD STORAGE PLAN:
Simple Charts for Quick Planning

While squirrels rely on instinct to tell them how many acorns to store, we, on the other hand, need to plan before we begin to gather our "acorns." The information in this section simplifies planning. The following charts become an organized "gathering" or shopping list.

Estimated Food Storage Needs Chart
▸ This chart is based on the following amounts. These provide the average adult with approximately 2300 calories per day for one year.

*Grains	300 lbs/person	Fat or oil	20 lbs/person
Sugar or honey	60 lbs/person	Dried legumes	60 lbs/person
		Garden Seeds	

From "Essentials of Home Production and Storage," Church of Jesus Christ of Latter-day Saints publication, 1978, pg.10

Salt   8 lbs/person (allows for bread making, preserving and medicinal needs.)

*Milk   about 50-100 lbs/person (see **Milk** pg. 25 for explanation)

*It is possible to store as little as 16 lbs. dried milk/person as long as the grains are increased to 400 lbs/person.

▸ The chart lists foods most commonly stored under each general category given above. The numbers next to each food on this chart are our estimates in pounds—tallied to reach the totals given above.
▸ To assist you in planning for more than one person, we have figured the quantities for 2, 3, 4 and 6 people in the columns across the chart.

Basic Food Storage Plan
▸ These planning sheets will assist you in making your own individualized plan. Planning for and buying the basic food storage items are your priority.
▸ For easy planning:
1. Begin planning by referring to the "Estimated Food Storage Needs" chart where the numbers are already figured for you. Find the column for the number of people in your family and copy, in pencil, the corresponding numbers for each item on to your "Basic Food Storage Plan" in "Total Quantity Needed".
2. On these planning sheets, total estimated amounts for oatmeal and pasta can be broken up between their different varieties in the spaces provided. To allow for personal preference and variety, there are blank spaces in each category for you to add additional favorite foods. Adding favorite foods within any category is simple—subtract pounds from one of the listed foods and record them beside the food you want to add. This keeps the total for each category the same.
3. Next, evaluate how the quantities fit with the tastes of your family and adjust the figures within each category accordingly. For example, if cornbread isn't a family

favorite but oatmeal is, you may lower the pounds of cornmeal and increase the pounds of oatmeal by the same amount. For optimum nutrition, 65% of the foods in the GRAIN category should be whole grains. Our recommended estimates are figured to represent this percentage. You will want to exchange whole grains with whole grains to maintain this proportion. You may make adjustments in all other categories, exchanging pounds for pounds, according to your family preferences.

▸ For simplicity, we recommend planning for all members of the family, including children, as though they were adults. This prevents the need to refigure quantities as children grow. For large families on a tight budget who are willing to go through the calculations, the following information is provided.

"Because children are growing, they need more food in proportion to their size than do adults. It's helpful to add two years to a child's current age when calculating adequate food storage amounts then, by knowing the number of children in a family and their ages, parents can estimate food needs as a percentage of an adult portion.

Age of Child	Percentage of Adult Portion
3 and under	50%
4-6	70%
7-10	90%
11 and up	100%

"Infants who are nursing share in their mother's portion. Keep in mind that young children, as well as pregnant and nursing mothers, need more milk than other family members.

"Food Storage needs for large families probably should be re-assessed yearly." Kay B. Franz, Associate Professor of Nutrition, Brigham Young University, *Ensign*, March 1998, pg. 71.

▸ Milk and oil have a short shelf life and must be rotated before they develop off flavors. Although we recommend planning for children as though they were adults, when it comes to milk and oil, *we recommend buying only those amounts that you can reasonably rotate within the shelf life.* By the time children reach teenage years, it will be practical to store and rotate the recorded adult amounts.

Expanded Basic Food Storage

▸ We have recommended a few essential expanded food storage items and estimated amounts. Storing these **greatly** increases the variety of recipes that can be prepared with basic food storage items. In addition to the basic food items, we consider these expanded foods a **priority**. These few items allow you make a greater variety of foods with grains and beans.

Important: As you fill out your basic and expanded food storage plans, it is important to read the following section entitled "Tips in a Nutshell: Basic Food Storage." These tips contain information and suggestions that will help you make informed decisions as you plan and purchase your food storage.

NOTE: It is possible to store as little as 16 lbs. dried milk/person as long as the grains are increased to 400 lbs/person. This option assists people who do not drink a lot of milk or who are on a very tight budget. Should you decide to do this, adjust the following figures accordingly.

ESTIMATED FOOD STORAGE NEEDS FOR ONE YEAR *All numbers indicate pounds unless otherwise specified.*						
Basic Food Storage						
ITEM	1 Person	2 People	3 People	4 People	5 People	6 People
GRAINS:	Quantities tabulated below represent required 65% *whole grains.					
Wheat*	135	270	405	540	675	810
Rolled Oats* (quick, regular)	30	60	90	120	150	180
Cornmeal*	30	60	90	120	150	180
Pearled Barley*	3	6	9	12	15	18
Rice, white	60	120	180	240	300	360
Enriched White Flour	12	24	36	48	60	72
Pasta	30	60	90	120	150	180
TOTAL GRAINS:	300	600	900	1200	1500	1800
LEGUMES: For canned beans, store 2½ times any part of dried bean quantities given below.	Two kinds of legumes are recorded per row.					
Dry Beans: Kidney / Red or Pink	16	32	48	64	80	96
Pinto / White	16	32	48	64	80	96
Lima / Black	6	12	18	24	30	36
Lentils / Split Peas	4	8	12	16	20	24
Legume ABC Soup Mix	16	32	48	64	80	96
Peanut Butter — is ½ protein & ½ fat. Only the protein portion is calculated in legume total. *(Total amount of peanut butter to store)*	2 (4)	4 (8)	6 (12)	8 (16)	10 (20)	12 (24)
TOTAL LEGUMES:	60	120	180	240	300	360

ESTIMATED FOOD STORAGE NEEDS FOR ONE YEAR (CONT.)
All numbers indicate pounds unless otherwise specified.

Basic Food Storage (cont.)

ITEM	1 Person	2 People	3 People	4 People	5 People	6 People
FATS & OILS:	Quantities below are expressed in pounds for ease in calculating TOTAL FATS & OILS.					
Vegetable Oil	8 or 1 gal.	16 or 2 gals.	24 or 3 gals.	32 or 4 gals.	40 or 5 gals.	48 or 6 gals.
Shortening—Regular or Butter Flavored (3 lb. can)	7.5 or 2½ cans	15 or 5 cans	22.5 or 7½ cans	30 or 10 cans	37.5 or 12½ cans	45 or 15 cans
Mayonnaise	1.5 or 1 qt.	3 or 2 qts.	4.5 or 3 qts.	6 or 4 qts.	7.5 or 5 qts.	9 or 6 qts.
Salad Dressing (Mayonnaise Type)	1 or 1 qt.	2 or 2 qts.	3 or 3 qts.	4 or 4 qts.	5 or 5 qts.	6 or 6 qts.
Peanut Butter—Fat portion of peanut butter is added here. *(For total amt. to store see LEGUMES)*	2	4	6	8	10	12
TOTAL FATS & OILS:	**20**	**40**	**60**	**80**	**100**	**120**
SUGARS:	Quantities below are expressed in pounds of sugar for ease in calculating TOTAL SUGARS.					
Granulated, white	28	56	84	112	140	168
Brown	5	10	15	20	25	30
Powdered Sugar	2	4	6	8	10	12
Honey	5	10	15	20	25	30
Corn Syrup	1.25 or 1 (16-oz.) jar	2.5 or 2 (16-oz.) jars	3.75 or 3 (16-oz.) jars	5 or 4 (16-oz.) jars	6.25 or 5 (16-oz.) jars	7.5 or 6 (16-oz.) jars
Molasses	.75 or 1 (12-oz.) jar	1.5 or 2 (12-oz.) jars	2.25 or 3 (12-oz.) jars	3 or 4 (12-oz.) jars	3.75 or 5 (12-oz.) jars	4.5 or 6 (12-oz.) jars
Maple Syrup	2.25 or 1 (36-oz.) jar	4.5 or 2 (36-oz.) jars	6.75 or 3 (36-oz.) jars	9 or 4 (36-oz.) jars	11.25 or 5 (36-oz.) jars	13.5 or 6 (36-oz.) jars
Jams & Preserves	2 or 2 pints	4 or 4 pints	6 or 6 pints	8 or 8 pints	10 or 10 pints	12 or 12 pints
Fruit Drink, powdered	13 or 2 (#10) cans	26 or 4 (#10) cans	39 or 4 (#10) cans	52 or 8 (#10) cans	65 or 10 (#10) cans	78 or 12 (#10) cans
Flavored Gelatin	1.25 or 3 (6-oz.) pkgs	2.5 or 6 (6-oz.) pkgs	3.75 or 9 (6-oz.) pkgs	5 or 12 (6-oz.) pkgs.	6.25 or 15 (6-oz.) pkgs.	7.5 or 18 (6-oz.) pkgs.
TOTAL SUGARS:	**60.5**	**121**	**181.5**	**242**	**302.5**	**363**

Basic Food Storage (cont.)

ITEM	1 Person	2 People	3 People	4 People	5 People	6 People
MILK: (See "Tips in a Nutshell: Basic Food Storage")	Quantity of powdered milk varies with mixing instructions, figures below are for 3 cups/day/person.					
Nonfat, Dry Milk Quantities vary depending on type and brand. See pg. 25 for options.	50 to 104	100 to 208	150 to 312	200 to 416	250 to 520	300 to 624
Evaporated Milk (12 fl. oz. can)	2 or 12 cans	4 or 24 cans	6 or 36 cans	8 or 48 cans	10 or 60 cans	12 or 72 cans
TOTAL MILK:	52 to 106	104 to 212	156 to 318	208 to 424	260 to 530	312 to 636
SALT: (Iodized)	8	16	24	32	40	48
MULTI-VITAMINS:	365 pills	730 pills	1095 pills	1460 pills	1825 pills	2190 pills
GARDEN SEEDS:	Quantities and Types Are Personal Preference					
WATER: 2 week supply	14 gals.	28 gals.	42 gals.	56 gals.	70 gals.	84 gals.

Expanded Basic Food Storage

ITEM	1 Person	2 People	3 People	4 People	5 People	6 People
Yeast, dry	1-2	2-4	3-6	4-8	5-10	6-12
Baking Soda	1	2	3	4	5	6
Baking Powder	2	4	6	8	10	12
Dried Eggs	1 #10 can	1 #10 can	1-2 #10 cans	1-2 #10 cans	2-3 #10 cans	2-3 #10 cans
Vanilla	Quantities Are Personal Preference					
Bouillon (beef, chicken, ham)						
Powdered Shortening (Record in Fats & Oils—See "Tips in a Nutshell: Expanded Basic Food Storage")	1 #10 can = 2 lbs. oil	1 #10 can = 2 lbs. oil	1 #10 can = 2 lbs. oil	1-2 #10 cans = 2-4 lbs. oil	1-2 #10 cans = 2-4 lbs. oil	1-2 #10 cans = 2-4 lbs. oil
Powdered Butter (Record in Fats & Oils—See "Tips in a Nutshell: Expanded Basic Food Storage")	1 #10 can = 2 lbs. oil	1 #10 can = 2 lbs. oil	1 #10 can = 2 lbs. oil	1-2 #10 cans = 2-4 lbs. oil	1-2 #10 cans = 2-4 lbs. oil	1-2 #10 cans = 2-4 lbs. oil

BASIC FOOD STORAGE PLAN

Extra spaces in each category are provided for additional food items you desire.

ITEM	Total Quantity Needed for _____ people	Amount on Hand	Quantity to Buy
GRAINS: (65% should be *whole grains)			
Wheat*			
Rolled Oats*: Quick/ Regular			
Cornmeal*			
Pearled Barley*			
Rice, white			
Enriched White Flour			
Pasta:			
TOTAL GRAINS:			

LEGUMES: For canned beans, store 2½ times any part of dried bean quantities.	Divide suggested amounts between the two legumes on each row according to your preference.		
Dry Beans: Kidney / Red or Pink	/	/	/
Pinto / White	/	/	/
Lima / Black	/	/	/
Lentils / Split Peas	/	/	/
Legume ABC Soup Mix			
Peanut Butter— is ½ protein & ½ fat. Only the protein portion is calculated in Legume total. (Total amount to store.)	( )	( )	( )
TOTAL LEGUMES:			

© 2003 Probert, Harkness, Emergency Food in a Nutshell, 2nd Edition, Revised

BASIC FOOD STORAGE PLAN (CONT.)

Extra spaces in each category are provided for additional food items you desire.

ITEM	Total Quantity Needed for _____ people	Amount on Hand	Quantity to Buy
FATS AND OILS:			
Vegetable Oil			
Olive Oil			
Shortening			
Mayonnaise			
Salad Dressing (Mayonnaise type)			
Peanut Butter—The fat portion is recorded here. *(For total amount to store see LEGUMES)*			
TOTAL FATS AND OILS:			
SUGARS:			
Granulated, white			
Brown			
Powdered Sugar			
Honey			
Corn Syrup			
Molasses			
Maple Syrup			
Jams & Preserves			
Fruit Drink, powdered			
Flavored Gelatin			
TOTAL SUGARS:			

BASIC FOOD STORAGE PLAN (CONT.)
Extra spaces in each category are provided for additional food items you desire.

ITEM	Total Quantity Needed for _____ people	Amount on Hand	Quantity to Buy
MILK:			
Nonfat, Dry Milk			
Evaporated Milk			
TOTAL MILK:			
SALT: (Iodized)			
Multi-Vitamins:			
GARDEN SEEDS:			
WATER: (2 week supply)			

EXPANDED BASIC FOOD STORAGE PLAN
These items are critically important for cooking with Basic Food Storage.

Yeast, dry			
Baking Soda			
Baking Powder			
Dried Eggs			
Vanilla			
Bouillon (beef, chicken, ham)			
Powdered shortening	If you store these items they should be recorded in FATS & OILS section. See "Estimated Food Storage Needs" chart for quantities and oil equivalents.		
Powdered butter			

© 2003 Probert, Harkness, Emergency Food in a Nutshell, 2nd Edition, Revised

TIPS IN A NUTSHELL: BASIC FOOD STORAGE

GRAINS*

- Store a variety of grains to keep food interesting and nutritious—65% should be whole grains. Very young children and older people can have a low tolerance for large amounts of whole wheat. It is important to store other grains and white flour to offer them milder options.
- Wheat—Hard Red and Hard White store best.
    - Look for wheat that has a protein content of at least 12%. This protein content forms enough gluten to make bread that rises well.
    - Look for wheat that has a moisture content of 12% or less to prevent growth of fungi and bacteria during storage.
    - Hard White (or Golden 86) is bred to make a lighter, in color, wheat product. For some, it is milder to the digestive system than red wheat.
    - Wheat stored at very high temperatures (in a shed) and then ground in to flour will not rise well in breads.
    - Since wheat packaged in #10 cans or buckets can be stored for up to 25 years, it is not necessary to rotate these containers on a regular basis. Instead, to save money, buy an inexpensive bag of wheat to use in day to day cooking. Wheat will last a very long time even after the bag is opened.
    - Some manufactures sell wheat in double-layer plastic bags designed for long term storage. (This will be specified on the package.) This packaging is usually less expensive than #10 cans or buckets. The danger in storing wheat this way, however, is that it is not safe from rodents. Wheat today is triple-cleaned making the presence of weevils extremely rare.
    - A Word about Wheat Grinders:

        Unless you store a wheat grinder, you will have no way of making whole wheat flour. An electric grinder is a great solution for busy people who want to include whole wheat in their family diet. However, in a time without electricity, a hand grinder is essential.

        When buying a hand grinder, consider not only the price but the turning ease, the fineness of the grind, and the speed in which it makes flour. Hand grinders employ a variety of burrs to make flour and vary greatly in cost, not always indicative of the ease of use or fineness of the flour produced.

        Stone burr grinders and some well-made iron/steel burr grinders make beautifully fine wheat flour. These usually require a great amount of time and energy to operate their very stiff turning action. They can take up to 10 minutes to grind about 1½ cups of flour. Back to Basics makes an inexpensive hand grain mill that produces slightly coarser flour in a much shorter time (about 3 min. to grind 1½ cups of flour). Children can easily operate this grinder.

        Save money to buy a grinder by eating nutritious food storage breakfasts (see Breakfasts—Recipe section) instead of boxed cereals. The average family

can save enough money each week to buy a hand grinder within about 3 months or an electric grinder in about a year!
  ► Brown rice contains fatty acids that cause it to go rancid rapidly. It will only store 6 months when exposed to air and 1-2 years in packages where the oxygen has been removed.
  ► Pasta—storing an assortment of different shapes and sizes add variety and interest to meals.

LEGUMES*

  ► Dried beans do not last indefinitely. Old beans require longer soaking and cooking times. Very old beans will not tenderize.
  ► In place of dried legumes:
   • Canned beans (also chili, baked beans, pork 'n beans, etc.) and canned split pea soup may be substituted for dried legumes. Dried legumes, when cooked, increase in size about 2½ times. Therefore, when storing canned legumes, store 2½ times the recommended dried amounts.
      — Canned or bottled legumes, when drained, can be gentler to the digestive system than cooked dried beans. Generally, these produce less gas.
      — Canned legumes save cooking time and fuel. While canned legumes are more expensive than dried, look for sales to save money.
      — 10 lbs. dried beans=32 (15 oz.) cans canned beans, excluding liquid.
      — For the money-saving benefits of storing dried beans plus the advantages of canned legumes, consider bottling dried beans yourself. This requires a pressure canner for safe bottling.
   • Canned meats may be substituted lb. for lb. for any part of dried legumes.
  ► Soup mix recommendations are generous on the "Estimated Food Storage Needs" chart because it is so quick and easy to fix and also very delicious.
  ► TVP (Textured Vegetable Protein) is an inexpensive meat substitute made from soy beans. 1 #10 can TVP (about 3 lbs.) Is the protein equivalent of about 7.5 lbs. dried legumes or about 15 lbs. canned legumes.

*A sudden change to a high-fiber diet including whole grains and legumes will make people feel ill. Though these foods store for a long time, it is important to include them in your family's regular diet so they are accustomed to them. High-fiber foods are a very healthy and nutritious addition to any menu.

FATS & OILS

  ► It is worth storing a good quality oil for its excellent flavor over time.
  ► Oils must be rotated carefully (within about a year) so they won't go rancid. Storing oils in a cool, dark place can extend the shelf life of high quality oils.
  ► Equivalents—The following will be helpful in figuring the total lbs. of oil stored in different forms:

1 gal. vegetable oil = 8 lbs. oil   1 qt. salad dressing (mayonnaise type) = 1 lb. oil
1 can shortening = 3 lbs. oil   1 lb. peanut butter = ½ lb. vegetable oil
1 qt. mayonnaise = 1.5 lbs. oil

- ▸ Vegetable oil—most of oil stored will be used in making bread. To check recommended total, choose family favorite bread recipe. Figure amount of oil needed based on how many loaves your family will eat/day x 365 days/year. Allow extra for fried foods.
  - The recommended amount of oil will be difficult to get through without making bread. For very busy people it is important to find fast bread recipes or invest in a breadmaker. Consult the Recipe section for fast bread recipes, or Appendix I for other recipes that rotate oil.
- ▸ Olive oil has a longer shelf life than vegetable oil. "Extra Virgin" and "Virgin" olive oil are darker and have a stronger flavor. "Extra Light" and "Light" olive oil will be lighter in color and flavor therefore making them a good option in baking.
- ▸ Olive oil has naturally occurring waxy molecules that tend to congeal and turn into white particles that float and sink to the bottom of the bottle when stored in cool temperatures. These are harmless and will disappear when oil is brought to room temperature. Olive oil is good to use until it develops a rancid odor.
- ▸ Crisco manufacturers used to say that Crisco shortening would store indefinitely if unopened and stored in a cool, dark place. However, they are currently only recommending a two year shelf life. Our recommendations for shortening amounts are generous because it can store well. If you can reliably rotate more liquid oil than we recommended, decrease the amount of shortening you store.
- ▸ Buy mayonnaise and mayonnaise-type salad dressing in small jars in case refrigeration is not available in an emergency.

SUGAR
- ▸ White sugar is less messy to use than honey.
  - Stores indefinitely if kept away from moisture.
  - Is less expensive than honey.
- ▸ Honey is sweeter than sugar—use less in cooking—messier to use.
  - Is more expensive than sugar.
  - Amount on "Estimated Food Storage Needs" chart _does not_ include honey for bread making. If you use honey in your bread, figure additional amount to store based on how many loaves your family will eat/day x 365 day/year. This additional honey can be exchanged lb. for lb. with white sugar.
  - 1 lb. honey = about 1⅓ c. honey
  - Not more nutritious than sugar—has a few trace minerals widely found in other foods.
  - Crystallizes—transfer bulk honey to new or used jars that can be easily heated to dissolve honey.
  - Over time darkens and develops slightly stronger taste; can eventually turn black.
  - Can contain a spore that is harmless to adults but can cause botulism in babies. For babies under one year old, use other sweeteners besides fresh honey.

Bread made with honey would be safe, as the spore is killed when exposed to the prolonged high heat of baking.

- ► Corn syrup—16 fl. oz. = about 1.25 lb. sugar
  - • Some may contain a spore that is harmless to adults but can cause botulism in babies. For babies under two years old, use other sweeteners.
- ► Molasses—12 fl. oz. = about ¾ lb. sugar
  - • High in iron—some like molasses on bread as well as using it in baking.
- ► Imitation Maple Syrup—36 fl. oz. = about 2.25 lbs. sugar
- ► Jams & Preserves—1 pint (2 cups) = about 1 lb. sugar
- ► Powdered Fruit Drink Mix—1 #10 can = about 6.5 lbs. sugar
  - • Includes Tang and powdered lemonade.
- ► Flavored gelatin—use for salads and desserts. Can also provide clear fluids during flu or diarrhea.
  - • 3 (6-oz.) pkgs. or 6 (3-oz.) pkgs. = about 1.25 lbs. sugar

MILK

- ► Dry milk is the most expensive item to acquire in basic food storage.
  - • Taste is a big issue. Choose a brand that your family will drink so you will use it and rotate it. Obtain samples if you can and serve mystery milk #1, #2 and #3. Let family vote so they will be willing to drink what you buy. If taste is still a problem, try adding a little vanilla.
  - • Quantities to store:
    Amounts vary depending on type (instant vs. non-instant) and brand of milk. Different types and brands require varying proportions of dry milk to water. The following information will help you figure the ideal amount of milk for your family.

    U S Recommended Daily Intake for:
    Children: 1-8 yrs. = 2 cups/day
    Young People: 9-18 yrs. = 4 cups/day
    Adults: 19-50 yrs. = 3 cups/day
    Adults: 51+ years = 4 cups/day
    (Average = about 3 c./day)

    Example: For 1 person 3 cups/day for 1 year = 50-100 lbs. depending on type and brand of dry milk.

  - • Some families do not use this much milk - 3 c./person/day. Adjust amount you store to what you will consume so you can rotate it within 3-5 years. *It is possible to store as little as 16 lbs. dried milk/person as long as the grains are increased to 400 lbs./person.*
  - • For best flavor, dry milk needs to be rotated within 3-5 years. Be aware that longer storage times and high temperatures can cause strong flavors to develop.
  - • Many non-instant brands are not fortified with vitamin A, which can be found in other foods that you store (See Tips in a Nutshell: Expanded Food Storage, Fruits & Vegetables). If milk is not fortified with Vitamin D make sure family, especially children, get out in the sun regularly.

- Milk Alternate (whey based dry milk) may require mixing in hot water. Mix desired amount in a small amount of hot water until dissolved. Add additional cold water to cool quickly. This milk cannot be used to make cheese, cottage cheese, or yogurt because it contains no milk solids.
  - Evaporated milk—6 (12 oz.) cans = 1 lb. dry milk

SALT
- Store iodized salt to provide essential iodine in diet.
- To preserve the unstable iodine, salt must be stored in a closed container.

SEEDS
- The least expensive way to store seeds of your choosing is in an opaque container with a lid in a cool, dark place. They may be kept in their original packages and then placed in a container. Stored this way they will last for a year.
- Older seeds will not all germinate. For additional information, *see* Appendix F.

WATER
- It is far better to store water now, while you have access to safe water supplies, before an emergency. Emergency treatment methods used on water from questionable sources cannot guarantee the same quality water as a supply of properly stored water. (*Emergency Water: Home Storage and Emergency Disinfection,* Utah Dept. Of Environmental Quality, Division of Drinking Water, May 1996).
- It is impossible to store a year's supply of water. Authorities recommend a 2 week supply—at *least* 14 gallons/person: 7 for drinking/cooking, 7 for other purposes such as personal hygiene, cleaning, and laundering. In hot climates, during times of intense heat or increased physical activity, people will consume more than this amount. You will also want to store more water if you are using many dehydrated or freeze-dried foods.
- Because of widespread pollution, water is often contaminated by microorganisms, bacteria, viruses and chemicals. Municipal water suppliers work to eliminate all of these contaminants making municipal water the safest and least expensive source of water to store.
- FEMA recommends, "If your local water is treated commercially by a water treatment utility, you do not need to treat the water before storing it. Additional treatment of treat public water will not increase storage life. If you have a well or public water that has not been treated, follow the treatment instructions provided by your public health service or water provider."
- National emergency authorities recommend <u>changing and replacing stored water every 6 months</u>.
- UNSAFE drinking water containers include:

- Water Beds—Algaecide and other chemicals in this water make it unsafe to use for drinking or cooking. In an emergency it can, however, be used for washing clothes.
- Bleach Bottles—are NOT safe for drinking and cooking water, but can store water for other purposes.
- Plastic Milk Containers—are biodegradable, develop leaks easily.
- SAFE water storage containers include:
  - 55-gallon, food grade plastic drums. *New* barrels are best for drinking water as they will not taint the water in any way and do not provide a residual food source for bacteria. Clean, *used* barrels could store water for washing clothes (about 460 lbs. when filled).
    — A 55-gallon drum can be emptied with a siphon pump or use a hose that is completely filled with water and while holding both ends up, to keep water in, quickly put one end all the way down to bottom of barrel, then lower other end to ground level and allow water to flow. (Using a new water hose, like those designed for use in recreation vehicles may be a clean idea for siphoning and filling.)
  - 5-gallon heavy duty plastic containers with spigot to dispense water (about 42 lbs. when filled).
  - 5 or 6 gallon Mylar water storage bags contained in cardboard boxes. These stack well (about 50 lbs. when filled).
  - 2-liter plastic drink bottles with screw-on cap, cleaned (about 3 lbs. when filled).
  - Insulated container like a thermos or cooler.
- FEMA recommends that containers to be used for storing water be rinsed with a diluted bleach solutions of 1 part bleach to 10 parts water before filling them.
- Store containers away from petroleum, insecticides, and anything else with a strong odor. Store containers in a dark place where any leakage will not cause damage. If water is stored in a location where freezing is possible, be sure to allow enough space in the top of the container for water expansion. (Freezing and subsequent thawing can cause calcium carbonate to distill out of water forming a film on the water surface. If your water has been properly stored and pre-treated, you can know that this film is harmless.)
- Stored water can taste flat after awhile. Aerate it by pouring it back and forth between two containers for a few minutes. This puts air back into the water which greatly improves the taste.
- Storing bottled water is an option.
  - While the FDA has not established a shelf life for bottled water, the International Bottled Water Association says that "Bottled water can be stored indefinitely if stored properly. Bottled water should be stored in a cool (ie. room temperature), dry environment, away from chemicals such as household cleaning products and away from solvents such as gasoline, paint thinners and other toxic materials."

- Commercial water service companies, such as Culligan, sell water bottled in large containers which they deliver to businesses and homes. Culligan recommends a storage life of about 3 years at which time they can deliver new bottles and take away the old.
- The American Red Cross cautions that bottled water should be changed and replaced every year. Once the seal is broken it should be used promptly.
- According to the University of California Berkeley, "Bottled water, in spite of its phenomenal popularity, may not be safer or more healthful than tap water. Some studies have found that tap water tends to have lower bacterial counts than bottled, and that some bottled waters are out of line with standards for tap water. Some bottles, however, are just packaged tap water."
- Bottled water is more expensive that storing tap water.

▶ *In an emergency, if you run out of stored water*, NO outside water source (including ground water or clear sparkling brook water) can be presumed safe. All water should be purified unless assured otherwise by competent local advice. If ever there is a choice, ground water is better to purify than surface water (lakes, rivers, streams). Water can be disinfected with one of the following methods. Boiling, chemical disinfection, and filtering do not remove toxic chemical contaminants already present in the water. Therefore, it is important to find water with the least possibility of chemical contamination to treat.

- BOILING. The SAFEST way of disinfecting water. It is effective in killing disease causing microorganisms present in water including cysts of giardia and cryptosporidium. If water is cloudy, strain through a clean cloth into a container before boiling.
  — According to the EPA, water must be boiled vigorously 1 minute. However, other emergency authorities say that water from questionable sources may need to be boiled for 3-5 minutes.
  — Water boils at lower temperatures with increasing altitudes. According to the Center for Disease Control, at altitudes above 6,562 feet (2 kilometers) boil water for 3 minutes which adds an extra margin of safety.
  — To improve the taste of boiled water, aerate by pouring it back and forth between two clean containers or add a pinch of salt per quart of boiled water. Some heat resistant organisms may survive the above boiling times but diseases caused by these organisms would be extremely rare. If sterile water is required, it should be heated in a pressure cooker at 250° F for 15 minutes.
- CHEMICAL DISINFECTION. When it is not feasible to boil water, chemical disinfection can be used.
  — The EPA says, "Chlorine and iodine are somewhat effective in protecting against exposure to Giardia, but may not be effective in controlling Cryptosporidium. Therefore, use iodine or chlorine only to disinfect well water (as opposed to surface water sources such as rivers, lakes and springs), because well water is unlikely to contain these disease causing organisms.

Chlorine is generally more effective than iodine in controlling Giardia, and both disinfectants work much better in warmer water."

— The American Red Cross, however, is saying, "The only agent to treat water should be household liquid bleach. Other chemicals such as iodine or water treatment products sold in camping or surplus stores that do not contain 5.25% sodium hypochlorite as the only active ingredient, are not recommended and should not be used."

— Chemical disinfectants are less effective in murky or cloudy water; filter it through a clean cloth or allow it to settle first. The colder the water, the longer the required time between addition of chemicals and use of the water.

— Liquid Chlorine Bleach (Unscented). Start by adding amounts recommended below. Bleach must be thoroughly mixed into the water and allowed to stand at least 30 minutes prior to using. A slight chlorine odor should be detected; if not, repeat the dosage and let stand an additional 15 minutes. If water has a strong chlorine taste, allow to stand exposed to the air for a few hours or pour between two clean containers.

    o   If water is cloudy, FEMA recommends doubling bleach dosage below.

    o   Liquid chlorine bleach loses strength over time—only bleach under one year old should be used to treat water. Double the dose for bleach 1-2 years old. Bleach over two years old should not be used.

Proportions of Water to Bleach The EPA, FEMA and CDC suggest the following: using 4-6% sodium chlorite (includes Clorox or Purex)	
Water	Bleach
1 Quart	2 drops
1 2-liter Bottle	4 drops
1 Gallon	8 drops (approx. ⅛ tsp.)
5 Gallons	40 drops (approx. ½ tsp.)
55 Gallon Drum	440 drops (approx. 5 tsp.)

- WATER FILTERS & PURIFIERS. Both can be effective as long as you have access to water. A water filter is essentially a strainer designed to remove microorganisms and bacteria. A purifier is a filter that additionally either removes viruses or kills them using some form of chemical disinfectant (e.g., iodine or chlorine).

  Contrary to some manufacturer claims, the EPA does not currently approve or test water filters/purifiers; however, they do offer manufacturers guidelines giving specific protocol for testing water filters/purifiers. For assurance on effectiveness of a filter/purifier in removing microorganisms, look for a certification by NSF(National Sanitation Foundation) Standard 53 or phone them at (800)673-8010 for a list of tested filters/purifiers.

A relatively inexpensive water filter with an absolute size of 1 micron or smaller will filter out giardia, cryptosporidium, and amoebas. If this water is then chemically disinfected, it will also be free of the most common enteric viruses.

It is *critical* to change the filters on both water filters and purifiers as directed or they will become clogged and reintroduce bacteria into the water. This is especially important with any filter containing carbon which is used to improve water taste, but can also be food for bacterial growth.

- OTHER SOURCES OF EMERGENCY WATER:
  Liquid in canned vegetables, fruits and fruit juices
  Canned or bottled drinks, and melted ice cubes
  After an emergency, *immediately turn off the water entering your home to prevent contamination*. Then the following sources of inside water can be used:
  Hot water heaters (turn off electricity or gas supply, then close cold
    water supply, open drain at bottom of tank, and turn on hot water faucet
    somewhere in house)
  Soft water tanks
  House pipes (open highest level faucet to then get water from lowest
    level faucet)
  Toilet tanks (not bowls). This water must be purified. However, do not
    use if chemical sanitizers have been used in the tank.

SOURCES FOR INFORMATION ON WATER:
    American Red Cross
    EPA (Environmental Protection Agency), Office of Water
    CDC (Center for Disease Control and Prevention)
    Central Utah Water Conservancy District
    The Department of Environmental Quality, State of Utah Division of Drinking Water
    FEMA (Federal Emergency Management Agency)
    National Sanitation Foundation, non-profit health organization, tests filters and
        bottled water. (800)673-8010 or www.nsf.org
    "Water" and "Water Filter Field Test," *Backpacker*, Dec. 1996, pg. 57-70, 112-13.

30

TIPS IN A NUTSHELL: EXPANDED BASIC FOOD STORAGE

YEAST, BAKING POWDER, BAKING SODA
- A good quality yeast in an unopened, foil package with all the oxygen removed (which will make the package hard and rectangular) will store at least 7 years in a deep freeze and 5 years in a refrigerator. Once opened, it will keep up to 1 year in a refrigerator.
- A 1-lb. pkg. yeast = about 29 T.
- Active dry yeast must be dissolved in warm water before adding it to a recipe. Instant yeast may also be dissolved in this way or, to speed things up, it can be added undissolved to a recipe with the flour. (Recipes in this book call for instant yeast.)
- The shelf life of Baking Powder can be extended by storing it in a cool, dark place.
- Substitution: 1 t. double acting baking powder (with shelf life) = ¼ t. baking soda (unlimited shelf life) + ⅝ t. cream of tartar (unlimited shelf life) *(Makes a single acting leavening substitute which, once moistened in a recipe, has to be put in the baking pan quickly and baked immediately.)*

DRIED EGGS
- One #10 can dried whole eggs contains around 100 eggs. Dried whole eggs should contain close to 100% dried egg solids rather than having multiple additives.
- 1 egg = 1 T. dried whole egg + 2 T. water
- Once opened, dried eggs will last about a year if stored in a cool, dry place. The heat of the drying process kills Salmonella bacteria.
- Though it is possible to make an egg substitute with gelatin for use in baking, we recommend storing and using dried eggs for their important nutritional value in a food storage diet.
- Egg Mix contains dried whole egg with dried milk. It is a substitute for scrambled eggs.

BOUILLON
- A good quality bouillon purchased in small containers at the grocery store last well if stored in a cool, dark place.
- Before buying any bouillon in bulk, obtain a taste sample. Some do not taste as "meaty," which can make a difference in food storage recipes that use little or no meat. Sometimes the extra money for a good bouillon is worth it.
- If you choose to store bouillon in a #10 can transfer to small jars with rubber-seal lids that will tighten well in order to preserve the flavor.

POWDERED SHORTENING

- 1 #10 can = about 11 c. powdered shortening. It is equal to about 2.25 cans regular shortening and has the caloric value of about 2 lbs. oil.
- 1 T. powdered shortening has ½ the calories of 1 T. regular shortening.
- Powdered shortening works well in quick mixes, but *does not* give good results in regular cake and cookie recipes. Because it is a powder, it combines quickly into the Super Quick Mix (*see Mixes—Recipe section*).

POWDERED BUTTER

- 1 #10 can = about 11 c. powdered butter. It is equal to about 8.25 lbs. real butter and has the caloric value of about 2 lbs oil.
- 1 T. powdered butter has ½ the calories of 1 T. fresh butter. It does not taste like fresh butter when hydrated.
- Powdered butter makes a fabulous white sauce/soup base but *does not* give good results in cakes and cookies. It does add flavor to recipes. Because it is a powder it combines quickly in the Super Quick White Sauce (*see Mixes—Recipe section*).
- Less expensive Powdered Margarine can be substituted for Powdered Butter with a sacrifice in flavor.

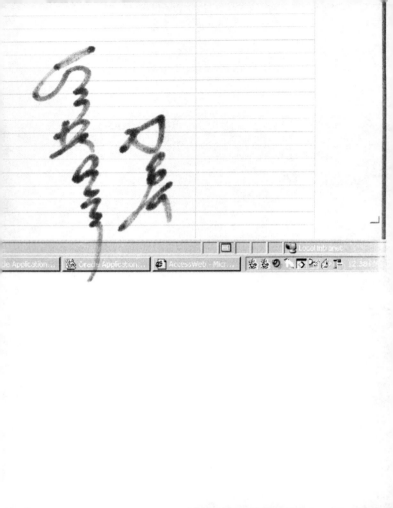

GATHERING CALENDAR: A YEARLY PURCHASING PLAN

Once you've made your food storage plan, it's time to start gathering "acorns." Feeling overwhelmed by the amount of food items to buy is typical. May we suggest dividing your buying strategy up into little "month-size" pieces. Start by simply gathering the items listed under the current month. After consulting your Food Storage Plan *buy what you can afford* (the BASICS are the priority). This calendar takes seasonal sales and availabilities into account. Dry milk and sugar are listed twice because they are the most expensive of the basic foods. Wheat, grains, and legumes are listed twice because of the large quantities you will need.

Though this book does not deal specifically with non-food items, they should not be forgotten. As December and January are not prime food-producing months in North America, we suggest gathering essential non-food items during these months.

At the end of the year, start the calendar again until you've acquired the amounts you've planned for. It is important to constantly pat yourself on the back because of what you <u>are</u> able to buy. Maintain your acquired supplies by replenishing them regularly.

Gathering Calendar	
JANUARY First-aid supplies and medications Personal and sanitary supplies Check clothing, blankets, and sewing supplies	**FEBRUARY** Oils & Fats: vegetable/olive oil, shortening, mayonnaise, salad dressing, etc. Dried Eggs
MARCH Vitamins Fruit Drink Mix (like Tang) Canned Meats	**APRIL** Salt:, iodized Garden Seeds Canned Vegetables and Fruits (sales) Water (rotate water and refill containers)
MAY Milk: dried, canned Baking Powder, Baking Soda Canned Vegetables and Fruits (sales)	**JUNE** Wheat & Grains: rice, oatmeal, pasta, etc. Legumes: dried, canned (summer sales)
JULY Sugar & Honey Dried Fruits and Vegetables (or dry/bottle your own)	**AUGUST** Sugar & Honey Dried Fruits and Vegetables (or dry/bottle your own)
SEPTEMBER Legumes: dried, canned Wheat & Grains: rice, oatmeal, pasta, etc.	**OCTOBER** Fuel: alternate cooking and heating supplies Paper items: toilet paper, tissues, etc. Water (rotate water and refill containers)
NOVEMBER Milk: dried, canned Yeast, Bouillon, Flavorings	**DECEMBER** Cleaning Supplies: soap, dish/laundry detergent Bleach or other disinfectants

© 2003 Probert, Harkness, <u>Emergency Food in a Nutshell, 2nd Edition, Revised</u>

HOW LONG WILL THESE ACORNS LAST ANYWAY?
SHELF LIFE INFORMATION

- The term "SHELF LIFE" suggests the amount of time that a food will maintain its optimum flavor, color, and nutrition.
- **Ideal storage conditions maintain the shelf life of stored foods.**
  Optimum storage conditions are: **Cool (70° F or lower)**
  Dark (in a basement)
  Dry
  High temperatures alone will decrease shelf life; cold temperatures can even extend it.
  Do not store food in hot places (garages, attics, storage sheds) if you can avoid it.
- **Ideal food packaging maintains the shelf life of stored foods.**
  Optimum storage containers are: **Opaque**
  Air-tight/moisture proof
  Oxygen depleted (low oxygen environment)
- Shelf life information is critical in helping you know how quickly you must rotate your food. After gathering the best expert information we could find from food manufacturers and distributors, we offer the following shelf life guidelines for food stored under the above conditions:

Basic Food Items	Best if Used Within
Sugar, Salt, Baking Soda	Indefinitely
Wheat	25 years
Legumes/Grains: White Rice, Pasta, Barley	8 years
Oats, Cornmeal, White Flour/Dry Milk Alternate	5 years
Dry Milk	3 to 5 Years
Oil/Garden Seeds	1 Year
Vitamins	See Container
Water	Rotate Every 6 Months

© 2003 Probert, Harkness, Emergency Food in a Nutshell, 2nd Edition, Revised

- Whole wheat, once ground, can last up to 3 months in normal household temperatures. Grinding whole wheat exposes oil in its outer coating to the air, making home ground whole wheat flour prone to going rancid. Commercial whole wheat flour stores for only 10-12 months in its package as purchased.

Expanded Food Items	Best If Used Within
Textured Vegetable Protein (TVP)	10 Years
Dried Vegetables Freeze-dried Fruits and Vegetables	8 Years
Dried Fruits Freeze-dried Meats	5 Years
Commercially Canned Fruits, Vegetables, Legumes and Meats, Dried Instant Potatoes Dried Eggs, Powdered Butter and Shortening	3 to 3½ Years
Canned Tuna Gluten Flour	2 Years
Canned or bottled fruit juices	1 to 2 Years
All other foods	6 Months to 5 Years*

© 2003 Probert, Harkness, <u>Emergency Food in a Nutshell, 2nd Edition, Revised</u>

*By using these foods regularly, you will know by experience how quickly they need to be rotated. This is easier than reading two or three pages of varying shelf life dates.

- Canned food experts such as Del Monte, Hormel, Canned Food Alliance and the USDA all say that canned foods will be safe to eat almost indefinitely as long as the cans are not bulging or dented. They suggest for optimum flavor, color and texture canned foods be consumed within 2-2½ years. The Canned Food Alliance says, "Food retains its safety and nutritional value well beyond two years, but it may have some variation in quality, such as a change of color and texture." To help you keep your sanity while rotating food storage, we have suggested a shelf life of 3-3½ years for canned foods.

- ***By eating food storage meals two days a week, an entire year's supply of food can be rotated in 3½ years!*** Everything can then be rotated within or close to its shelf life. (The exceptions are oil, tuna, and juices which have a shorter shelf life.)

- <u>As a general rule, after nitrogen packed containers are opened, most food will last a year or more</u>, at normal room temperatures, until it can be entirely used. The exception is dry milk, which should be used relatively quickly once opened for optimum flavor.

- Shelf life recommendations are not magic cut-off times. If you go beyond the suggested shelf life, don't worry. There is still plenty of nutrition left in the food. Open it and start using it. If there is no off smell or strange color, it will still be okay to use. Keep in mind that cooler storage temperatures increase shelf life.

For more information on Expanded Food Storage see the following section "Off and Running — Getting to the Finish Line." For convenience both Basic and Expanded shelf life information are kept in this section.

OFF AND RUNNING—GETTING TO THE FINISH LINE
What You Store = What You Eat

Storing additional items besides the Basics is important for two reasons. With these items the Basic foods can be served in many delicious ways instead of a limited few. They also make it possible for food storage dishes to taste more like those you are accustomed to eating. Consider the following:

If I store:
wheat, oats, rice, other grains
powdered milk
sugar or honey
oil
salt
dried legumes
water
garden seeds
vitamins

I can make:
cooked wheat, cracked wheat, oatmeal, rice, and other grains
creamed rice
unleavened bread
tortillas
cooked beans
sprouted beans and wheat

If I add to my storage:
yeast
baking soda
baking powder
dried whole eggs
vanilla
bouillon

Now I can make:
breads
biscuits, muffins
pancakes, French toast
cookies, cakes
puddings
simple soups with beans

If I add to my storage:
canned fruits and vegetables
dried fruits and vegetables
canned meats
spices and condiments

powdered butter

powered shortening

Now I can make:
more versatile soups
casseroles
salads

Super Quick White Sauce Mix –
    cream sauces and creamy soup base
Super Quick Mix –
    fast way to make pancakes, muffins and desserts

MAKING YOUR EXPANDED FOOD STORAGE PLAN:
Simple Charts for Quick Planning

The simplest way to organize Expanded Food Storage is to plan around the recipes you decide to serve. This ensures that you will have the essential ingredients needed for tasty dishes. It also helps you avoid buying foods in quantities that you won't use.

You will want recipes that use only stored foods. Food storage recipes that rely on a ham hock, sour cream, cheese and other fresh ingredients for good flavor are useless in an emergency when you may not have access to these foods. It is also important to search out a variety of recipes to keep food storage recipes interesting and appealing. This book contains over 200 fast and delicious, family-tested recipes using only stored foods. These include main dishes for 2 months using beans/legumes (dried, canned) and canned meats.

Follow these steps to plan your Expanded Food Storage:

1. Find food storage recipes for main dishes that you like and record them on the Favorite Food Storage Recipe List that follows. (Try each of these recipes first to confirm that you like them.)
2. Decide how many times per year you will serve each recipe and record it in the next column. Take into account seasonal menu changes.
3. In the last column, briefly list expanded food items needed for each recipe beyond the Basic foods. (Basic Food Storage ingredients have already been planned for in your Basic Food Storage Plan on the previous pages.)
4. Using this brief list, record the expanded food items and tally the amounts needed for a year's worth of your selected recipes on the succeeding charts provided. These charts become a simple shopping list and inventory record.

Be sure to plan for breakfasts, lunches and dinners. After you've collected your recipes and planned for expanded ingredients, you will be ready to plan for complete meals. The blank calendar found at the end of this section may be helpful. (Keep in mind it is ideal to have at least 5 servings/day of canned, dried, or freeze-dried fruits and vegetables.) See example menu-calendar in Appendix C.

FAVORITE FOOD STORAGE RECIPE LIST		
Recipe Title	# times/year	Briefly list food items needed beyond the Basics.

FAVORITE FOOD STORAGE RECIPE LIST (CONT.)

Recipe Title	# times/year	Briefly list food items needed beyond the Basics.

CANNED FRUITS AND VEGETABLES

ITEM	Tally Total Quantity Needed	Amount on Hand	Quantity to Buy
Apples, sauce			
Apricots			
Mandarin Oranges			
Peaches			
Pears			
Pineapple, chunks			
crushed			
Beans, green			
Carrots			
Corn, whole kernel			
creamed			
Peas			
Potatoes, sliced			
Tomatoes, diced			
paste			
sauce			
spaghetti sauce			

DRIED AND FREEZE-DRIED FRUITS AND VEGETABLES			
ITEM	Tally Total Quantity Needed	Amount on Hand	Quantity to Buy
Apples, sliced			
Apricots			
Prunes			
Raisins			
Beans, green			
Broccoli			
Cabbage			
Carrots, diced/sliced			
Celery, diced/sliced			
Corn			
Green Pepper			
Onions, diced			
Peas			
Potatoes, diced/sliced			
instant			
Tomatoes			

CANNED MEATS

Tip: Canned meats may be substituted lb. for lb. for legumes in Basic Food Storage. If you desire, add up the lbs. of meat you store and subtract them from the lbs. of legumes recorded on your Basic Food Storage Plan.

ITEM	Tally Total Quantity Needed	Amount on Hand	Quantity to Buy
Beef, chipped			
Beef, corned			
Beef, roast, chunks			
Chicken, chunks			
whole			
Clams			
Ham			
Salmon			
Spam			
Tuna			
Turkey, chunks			

ADDITIONAL EXPANDED FOOD STORAGE ITEMS
Include spices here.

ITEM	Tally Total Quantity Needed	Amount on Hand	Quantity to Buy

ADDITIONAL EXPANDED FOOD STORAGE ITEMS (CONT.)

ITEM	Tally Total Quantity Needed	Amount on Hand	Quantity to Buy

Plan–Your–Own Menu Calendar

Four Week Menu

Sunday	Monday	Tuesday	Wednesday	Thursday	Friday	Saturday
B: L: D:	B: L: D:	B: L: D:	B: L: D:	B: L: D:	B: L: D:	B: L: D:
B: L: D:	B: L: D:	B: L: D:	B: L: D:	B: L: D:	B: L: D:	B: L: D:
B: L: D:	B: L: D:	B: L: D:	B: L: D:	B: L: D:	B: L: D:	B: L: D:
B: L: D:	B: L: D:	B: L: D:	B: L: D:	B: L: D:	B: L: D:	B: L: D:

Plan–Your–Own Menu Calendar
Five Week Menu

Sunday	Monday	Tuesday	Wednesday	Thursday	Friday	Saturday
B: L: D:	B: L: D:	B: L: D:	B: L: D:	B: L: D:	B: L: D:	B: L: D:
B: L: D:	B: L: D:	B: L: D:	B: L: D:	B: L: D:	B: L: D:	B: L: D:
B: L: D:	B: L: D:	B: L: D:	B: L: D:	B: L: D:	B: L: D:	B: L: D:
B: L: D:	B: L: D:	B: L: D:	B: L: D:	B: L: D:	B: L: D:	B: L: D:
B: L: D:	B: L: D:	B: L: D:	B: L: D:	B: L: D:	B: L: D:	B: L: D:

45

TIPS IN A NUTSHELL: EXPANDED FOOD STORAGE

FRUITS & VEGETABLES

- U.S. Recommended Daily Allowances:
  - Fruits: 2-4 servings (½ c. ea.)/day/person
  - Vegetables: 3-5 servings (½ c. ea.)/day/person
- To get the most nutrition for your money, consider storing and/or planting the following in your garden. The ideal is at least 1 serving of foods rich in both Vitamin A and C each day.

Rich in Vitamin A	
Dark green leafy or orange vegetables and fruit	
apricots	lettuce (outside leaves)
peaches	parsley
nectarines	pumpkin
spinach	carrots
asparagus	squash
beets	sweet potato
broccoli	tomatoes

Rich in Vitamin C	
citrus fruits	broccoli
cantaloupe	cabbage
pineapple	cauliflower
strawberries	potatoes
juices enriched w/C	red & green peppers
tomatoes	

- For those worried about the nutrition in canned foods, the University of California, Berkeley says, "Fresh veggies and fruits [purchased in a grocery store] are not always the most nutritious, since many are harvested before they're ripe, trucked thousands of miles, and stored for long periods—in which case nutrient loses can be substantial. Thanks to improved technology, canned foods retain most of the food's vitamins and minerals. The heating process of commercial canning partly destroys some vitamins, but some nutrient loss is inevitable whenever food is prepared."
- Canned food experts such as Del Monte, Hormel, Canned Food Alliance and the USDA all say that canned foods will be safe to eat almost indefinitely as long as the cans are not bulging or dented. They suggest for optimum flavor, color and texture canned foods be consumed within 2-2½ years. The Canned Food Alliance says, "Food retains its safety and nutritional value well beyond two years, but it may have some variation in quality, such as a change of color and texture." To help you keep your sanity while rotating food storage, we have suggested a shelf life of 3-3½ years for canned foods.
- The acid in tomatoes and tomato products will react over time with the metal of the can causing the contents to spurt from the can when opened. As long as the can was not bulging prior to opening and has been stored at reasonable household

temperatures, it is still safe to use. Store brand/generic brand tomato sauce may not store 3 years without bulging. National brand tomato sauce stores better, probably because of better quality cans.

- Bulging cans of fruit or vegetables are NEVER safe to eat. Dented cans should not be stored. Dents may compromise the integrity of the seal, making food unsafe.
- Buy canned foods from stores that move food quickly. Fast turnover rates ensure that canned goods are as new as possible.
- Dried fruit is very high in iron, especially if it is dried uncooked. It is an important addition to food storage.
- Dried celery and dried green pepper greatly enhance the flavor of food storage recipes and are well worth the investment. You may have to shop around to find these more unusual dried vegetables. Freeze-dried forms of these foods do not retain flavor as well as dried when added to a recipe.
- Be aware that while freeze-dried fruits and vegetables taste great, you will add double the amount of the dried equivalent in any recipe because freeze-dried foods do not shrink as much in the drying process. Therefore, you will need to store double what you would store in dried fruits and vegetables.
- Freeze-dried peas are a great way to add some bright green color to food storage recipes. Because they hydrate quickly, they can be added toward the end of a recipe and still retain their flavor.
- We recommend fruits and vegetables be stored in addition to basic food storage items. If you desire, you may decrease the amounts of SUGARS, FATS & OILS stored on the "Basic Food Storage Plan" to compensate for the additional calories added from fruits and vegetables.

CANNED MEATS

- U.S. Recommended Daily Allowance = 2 servings/day/person
- According to the USDA, canned meats should be consumed within 2-5 years. We have suggested a shelf life of 3 years for canned meats with the exception of canned tuna which can develop off flavors after 2 years.
- Canned meats save cooking time and fuel.
- Buy from stores that move food quickly. Fast turnover rates ensure that canned goods are as new as possible.
- Ingredients on labels are listed according to quantity from largest to smallest. Look for cans that list meat first, even in the title. Be aware that canned "Gravy and Beef" will have more gravy than beef.
- Canned meats can replace any or all dried legumes on the "Basic Food Storage Plan" lb. for lb.
- Are more expensive than legumes. Eating legumes a few times a week can offset this cost.
- Bottled pre-cooked bacon pieces, available at the grocery store, have a shelf life of 3 years. Bacon adds important flavor to food storage recipes.

- Freeze-dried meats are a good food storage item, but are very expensive in comparison to canned meats. Because they do not contain water, it is difficult to offer accurate pound for pound conversions with legumes. Record these meats in the "Additional Expanded Food Storage Items" chart if you decide to store them.

CHEESE

- Powdered Cheese and Cheese Sauces vary widely and tend to loose their flavor when added to other foods, even macaroni.
- Old English Processed Sharp Cheese Spread is excellent way to have cheese flavor in food storage dishes. It is very salty—reduce salt in any possible place when included in a recipe. Bottled Processed Cheese stores indefinitely if stored in a cool, dark place. Most recipes require only ¼ to ½ (5-oz.) jar.
- Bottled Processed Sharp Cheese Spread, according to the University of California, Berkeley, last indefinitely (if stored in a cool, dark place). It retains a very good cheese flavor in foods. Eliminate or reduce salt in a recipe when adding this cheese to compensate for its high salt content.
- Freeze-dried sharp cheddar cheese has an excellent flavor and works best when hydrated and sprinkled on top of a dish to be baked. If added to a soup or stew it tends to stick badly on the bottom of the pan. It is expensive but is a great substitute for freshly grated cheese when used in baking.
- Cheese powder is cheese in powdered form. It can be added directly to recipes or made into a cheese sauce with water; add a little flour if needed to thicken or if flavor is too strong. Be sure you taste a sample before buying to make sure you like the flavor.
- Cheese Sauce Mix contains cheese powder plus white sauce ingredients. It will thicken when added to water and cooked. White sauce ingredients tend to dilute the cheese flavor, resulting in a weaker cheese taste when combined with other foods, even macaroni.
- Cheese Blend usually has blue cheese in it, probably to overcome the problem of flavor loss when combined with other foods. It usually has white sauce thickening ingredients.
- Record this food item on the Additional Expanded Food Storage Items chart. Figuring the milk equivalent for cheese can be too complicated.

(For resources on canning, bottling or drying, contact your state University Extension Service usually listed in the county government section of your phone book or look for a land grant university in your state.)

FAST AND DELICIOUS RECIPES:
Made Only with Stored Foods

This unique collection contains 200 recipes including two months of main dish recipes using beans/legumes (dried or canned) and canned meats. We have carefully chosen recipes that are delicious, easy to prepare, and fuel efficient. Directions have been altered wherever possible to reduce cooking and preparation times.

These recipes provide a variety of appetizing and nutritious meals that don't depend on fresh eggs, butter, margarine or cheese to taste good. All ingredients are storable foods. The recipes use simple lists of ingredients to minimize the number of foods to store. Where canned foods are used, salt has been reduced or eliminated.

ALL of these recipes can be prepared in an emergency with minimal equipment. Even the bread, cookie, and cake recipes can be easily cooked in an Applebox Reflector Oven with the same results as a conventional oven! (Instructions for this oven can be found at the end of Appendix D.)

Key:
t. = teaspoon
T. = tablespoon
c. = cup

See Appendix B for helpful information on cooking dried beans/legumes, hydrating dried foods, recipe substitutions, or general information, using food storage items.

Breakfasts

By eating food storage breakfasts, it is possible to save enough money to purchase a hand or electric wheat grinder within a few months time. The key to enjoying food storage breakfasts it to serve a variety.

Creamy Cracked Wheat

3 c. water
¼ c. dry milk (optional)

1 rounded c. cracked wheat (sifted if home ground)
¾ t. salt

Stir dry milk into water if desired. Bring water to boil, stir in rest of ingredients. Bring back to a boil, stirring. Cover and simmer on low for 20 minutes. Serve with milk and white or brown sugar. Serves 4-5.

Cooked Whole Wheat

Cook whole wheat in double the water for 1½ hours or to desired tenderness in saucepan. Serve topped with fruit, honey and cinnamon or stir in peanut butter, honey and a little water.

Thermos Wheat

2 c. water   1 c. whole wheat kernels

In small saucepan, bring water to boil. Pour about ½ cup boiling water into a 2-cup thermos. Cover and set aside. In sieve, wash wheat under running water. Pour hot water from thermos. Spoon washed wheat into hot thermos. Add remaining boiling water to about 1-inch from top of thermos. Attach lid. Let stand 6 hours or overnight. Serve topped with fruit, honey and cinnamon or stir in peanut butter and honey plus a little bit of water. Makes about 2 cups.

Other Cooked Cereal Ideas: Oatmeal, 6 or 9 Grain Cereal, Cream of Wheat (or Germade), Cornmeal Mush, Grits

Super Quick Pancakes

3½ c. Super Quick Mix, pg. 53   2 T. dried whole egg, sifted
1½ T. sugar   2¾ c. water

Whisk together dry ingredients. Add water and whisk just until combined (leave a few small lumps). Let stand 5 minutes. Cook on hot, oiled griddle. Makes 12, 6-inch pancakes.

Whole Wheat Pancakes

2 c. reconstituted dry milk   2 t. baking powder
2 T. bottled lemon juice or white vinegar   1 t. soda
2 c. whole wheat flour   ½ t. salt
2 T. dried whole egg, sifted   2 T. oil
1 T. sugar

Mix milk and lemon juice or vinegar together; let stand for 5 minutes. Mix dry ingredients together; add milk and oil. Whisk until smooth. Pour ⅓ cup amounts onto hot, greased griddle. Turn pancakes as soon as they are puffed and full of bubbles. Makes 10, 6-inch pancakes. *Make your own mix* by combining together 5 times the above dry ingredients. Store in airtight container. Measure 2¼ c. mix for each recipe above.

Fruit Syrup

Puree 1 can/bottle fruit, drained, reserving liquid. Add enough liquid back to fruit until for desired consistency.

German Pancakes

1 c. whole wheat flour
3 T. dried whole egg, sifted
2 T. sugar
¼ t. baking powder

1 c. reconstituted dry milk
⅔ c. water
1 t. vanilla
oil

Whisk together dry ingredients; add liquid ingredients and beat 1 min. Cook large pancakes one at a time in a 8- to 9-inch heavy skillet on medium heat. Swirl about ⅓ c. batter around in heated and oiled pan. Turn when lightly browned on the edges and dry on the top. Remove from pan when second side is lightly browned. Hold pancakes on plate in warm oven until they are all cooked. Spread jam on warm pancakes and sprinkle with cinnamon; roll and eat with fingers! Makes 7-8 pancakes.

Lemon Syrup: Stir together bottled lemon juice and powdered sugar. Add sugar until desired consistency.

Apple Pancakes

1 c. hydrated dried apple slices
  (hydrate in apple juice)
2 c. Super Quick Mix (pg. 53)

1 T. dried whole egg, sifted
½ t. cinnamon
1½ c. water

Whisk together dry ingredients. Drain apples, reserving juice; chop finely. Add apples and water to dry ingredients; whisk just until combined. Let stand 5 minutes. Cook in hot oiled griddle (these take a little longer to cook.) Makes 10, 4-inch pancakes.

Cider Syrup:

½ c. sugar
1 T. cornstarch
½ t. cinnamon

⅛ t. nutmeg
1 c. apple juice, including reserved juice above.
1 T. bottled lemon juice

In a small saucepan, whisk together dry ingredients. Add juice and bring to boil, stirring. Remove from heat; stir in lemon juice. Serve over Apple Pancakes.

Cornmeal Pancakes

1 c. cornmeal
3 T. sugar
1 T. dried whole egg, sifted
1 t. salt
1 c. boiling water

½ c. reconstituted dry milk
2 T. oil
½ c. flour
2 t. baking powder

Combine cornmeal, sugar, egg and salt. Slowly stir in boiling water, cover and let stand 8-10 minutes. Stir in milk and oil. Combine flour and baking powder; stir into cornmeal mixture with a few strokes. Do not beat. Cook on warm, lightly greased griddle. Yields about 12.

French Toast

1 c. reconstituted dry milk	½ t. vanilla
6 T. dried whole egg, sifted	¾ t. cinnamon (optional)
¼ t. sugar	¼ t. nutmeg (optional)
¼ t. salt	6-10 slices whole wheat or white bread, depending on absorbency

Beat all ingredients except bread together. Pour into a pie pan. Dip each slice of bread in egg mixture and fry in oiled pan. Serve with cinnamon sugar or syrup.

Fruit Muffins

2¾ c. Super Quick Mix, pg. 53	1 c. water (for pineapple, include juice in this water)
½ c. sugar, scant	1 c. crushed pineapple, drained OR 1 c. applesauce
1 T. dried whole egg, sifted	OR 1 (15 oz.) can blueberries, drained
	½ t. cinnamon (for applesauce muffins)

Whisk together dry ingredients. Add water and fruit; stir with spoon just until ingredients are moistened. Spoon batter into greased muffin pans. They will be very full. Bake at 400° F for 15-18 minutes. Makes 12 muffins (cupcake size).

Dried Apple Muffins*:* Soak ¾ c. dried apples in 1½ cups water or apple juice for 30 minutes. Drain, saving liquid, and chop apples. Combine dry ingredients above using entire ½ c. sugar. Add chopped apples and increase liquid (water or apple juice) to 1½ c. (include soaking liquid).

Fresh Fruit Variation: Add 1½ c. chopped fresh fruit in place of canned fruit. Add entire ½ c. sugar and ¼ t. cinnamon, if desired.

Muffins, Cornmeal and Magnificent, Orange and Oatmeal (pg. 58)

Basic Granola

To make this less expensive, coconut, almonds or sesame seeds can be replaced with more rolled oats.

6¼ c. rolled oats	½ c. vegetable oil
1 c. coconut	¾ c. honey
1 c. slivered almonds	1 t. vanilla
¼ c. sesame seeds	1 c. dried fruit (optional)
½ t. salt	

Stir dry ingredients together in large bowl. Mix oil and honey together; heat until honey is warm and runny. Stir in vanilla. Add to dry ingredients; stir until combined. Spread on 2 cookie sheets. Bake at 300° F for 20 minutes until lightly browned, stirring every 5 minutes during baking. Add dried fruit *after* cooled and store in air tight container. Keeps for 2-3 weeks.

For a low fat diet*:* omit oil, honey, vanilla, and salt and add brown sugar to mix. Eat ingredients raw without baking.

Mixes

These mixes are very fast to make because all ingredients are powdered. They are less expensive than ready-made mixes, help rotate powdered milk and leavening, and are a delicious way to eat whole wheat.

Super Quick Mix

9 c. fine whole wheat flour
9 c. white flour
3 c. instant dry milk
2½ c. powdered shortening, sifted
9 T. baking powder

2½ T. salt
1½ T. sugar
4 t. cream of tartar
2 t. baking soda

In a large bowl, combine ingredients well. Store in covered container. Label and date; use within 10-12 weeks. Makes about 24 cups.
For regular non-instant dry milk: add an additional 6 T. dry milk to mix above.
Variation: This mix can be made using all whole wheat flour; increase baking powder to 10 T.

Favorite Roll Mix

9 c. whole wheat flour
9 c. white flour
1 c. sugar

1 c. instant dry milk
2 T. salt

Mix all ingredients together well in a large bowl. Store in a cool dry place in an airtight container. Label and date; use within 10-12 weeks. Makes about 20 cups of mix.
For regular non-instant dry milk: add an additional 2 T. to mix above.
Variation: This mix can be made with all whole wheat flour.

Super Quick White Sauce Mix

4 c. instant dry milk
4 c. powdered butter, sifted
4 c. flour

8 t. chicken bouillon
2 t. salt

Mix above ingredients together, store in covered container, label and date. Use within 4-6 months. (Unbleached white flour makes a slightly thinner sauce; increase sauce mix in recipes.)

Thin white sauce	Medium white sauce	Thick white sauce
1 c. warm water	1 c. warm water	1 c. warm water
⅓ c. white sauce mix	½ c. white sauce mix	¾ c. white sauce mix

Whisk white sauce mix into water. Continue stirring over medium-high heat until boiling. Lower heat and simmer 1 minute. If needed, hold sauce for a short time on *low heat.*
Bechamel sauce: Add ¼ t. of onion powder and 1 bay leaf to mixture before bringing to boil. Remove bay leaf after simmering sauce 1 minute.
Parsley sauce: Add 1 t. to 1 T. dried parsley before simmering.
Cream Soup Base: This mix can be used as a cream soup base in any cream soup recipe.

Breads

Yeast Breads: *To make moist whole wheat bread that rises well add the least amount of flour possible and keep the dough as warm as possible throughout the entire process. Water that is too hot will kill yeast; too cold, the dough will not rise. White wheat makes a lighter colored bread.*

Gluten is natural protein derived from wheat. It is used in bread to provide elasticity and strength, added texture and helps retain moisture in bread and doughs. It helps prevent crumbling and extends the shelf life of baked bread. If you do not want to store gluten flour, <u>you may substitute whole wheat flour in its place.</u>

IN AN EMERGENCY, breads can be baked in an Applebox Reflector Oven, see pg. 142. Let bread rise in oven with 3-5 lit charcoal. When ready to bake, lift oven box just enough to slide in and spread out newly lit charcoals to reach baking temperature. If box is totally removed, bread will fall when exposed to cold air.

IMPORTANT NOTE: To make a 2-loaf recipe of bread #1 or #2 every other day for 1 year (1 loaf/day), you will need 275 lbs.(#1) or 366 lbs.(#2) of wheat ground into flour, 4 gallons of oil, 46 lbs. honey or sugar, 8 (1-lb.) pkgs. yeast, 61 c. gluten flour, 3⅔ qts. of lemon juice or 4 (21-oz.) cans dough enhancer, and 7.3 lbs. salt.

Easiest Whole Wheat Bread #1

Lemon juice in this recipe acts as a dough enhancer which gives bread a fine, light texture.

2 (8x4-inch) Loaves	4 (8x4-inch) Loaves
3½ c. whole wheat flour	7 c. whole wheat flour
⅓ c. gluten flour, sifted	⅔ c. gluten flour, sifted
1¼ T. instant yeast	2½ T. instant yeast
2½ c. steaming hot tap water (120-130° F)	5 c. steaming hot tap water (120-130° F)
1 T. salt	2 T. salt
⅓ c. oil	⅔ c. oil
⅓ c. honey or ½ c. sugar	⅔ c. honey or 1 c. sugar
1¼ T. bottled lemon juice	2½ T. bottled lemon juice
2½ c. whole wheat flour	5 c. whole wheat flour

Mix together first three ingredients in mixer with a dough hook. Add water all at once and mix for 1 minute; cover and let rest for 10 minutes. Add salt, oil, honey or sugar and lemon juice and beat for 1 minute. Add last flour, 1 cup at a time, beating between each cup. Beat for about 6-10 minutes until dough pulls away from sides of the bowl. This makes a very soft dough.

Pre-heat oven for 1 minute to lukewarm and turn off. Turn dough onto oiled counter top; divide, shape into loaves and place in oiled bread pans. Let rise in warm oven for 10-15 minutes until dough reaches top of pan. Do not remove bread from oven; turn oven to 350° F and bake for 30 minutes. Remove from pans and cool on racks.

If you do not have a mixer with a dough hook and are kneading this by hand, gradually add last cup of flour to keep dough from sticking to counter. You will add more flour when kneading by hand than when using a mixer simply to be able to handle this moist dough. With wheat bread, always add the least amount of flour possible to keep bread moist. Knead 10 minutes before shaping dough into loaves.

—Adapted recipe from Jamie Rasmussen

Easiest Whole Wheat Bread #2

Optional dough enhancer in this bread gives it a very fine, light texture and preserves moistness. Dough Enhancer has a shelf life of about 3 years. A 21-oz. can contains 4½ c. and makes the above (4-loaf) recipe 24 times. The 4-loaf recipe can also be made into 3 loaves and one 8-inch round cake pan of rolls or 2 loaves and one, 9x13-inch pan of rolls if desired.

2 (8x4-inch) Loaves
⅓ c. oil
⅓ c. honey or ½ c. sugar
2¼ t. salt
2¾ c. steaming hot tap water (120-130° F)
¼ c. gluten flour, sifted
1½ T. dough enhancer
1¼ T. instant yeast
7-8 c. whole wheat flour

4 (8x4-inch) Loaves
⅔ c. oil
⅔ c. honey or 1 c. sugar
1½ T. salt
5½ c. steaming hot tap water (120-130° F)
½ c. gluten flour, sifted
3 T. dough enhancer
2½ T. instant yeast
14-16 c. whole wheat flour

Mix together first four ingredients in mixer with a dough hook. Add ½ of flour and beat. Put in 1-2 more cups of flour, gluten flour, dough enhancer and yeast. Beat again. With mixer on medium speed, add remaining flour just until dough pulls away from the sides of the bowl. Knead 6-10 minutes on medium-high speed.

Pre-heat oven for 1 minute to LUKE WARM and turn off. Spray or oil pans. Pour dough out onto oiled counter, divide and shape into loaves and put into pans. Let loaves rise 35 minutes in warmed oven. Do not remove bread from oven; turn oven to 350° F and bake for 30 minutes. Tip out of pans and cool on cooling rack.

If you do not have a mixer with a dough hook and are kneading this by hand, gradually add last cup of flour to keep dough from sticking to counter. You will add more flour when kneading by hand than when using a mixer simply to be able to handle this moist dough. With wheat bread, always add the least amount of flour possible to keep bread moist. Knead 10 minutes before shaping dough into loaves.

—Adapted recipe from Johanne Perry

Easiest Whole Wheat Bread #3

3½ c. hot water
1 (12-oz.) can evaporated milk
⅔ c. oil
1 c. honey or 1½ c. sugar

1½ T. salt
12-14 c. whole wheat flour
1 c. gluten flour, sifted
3 T. instant yeast

Combine first five ingredients in bowl. Add half of the flour, gluten flour, and the yeast to wet mixture. (Do not put gluten flour in first because it will lump.) Mix until flour is just moistened. Let it set for a few minutes to develop yeast and gluten. Add remaining flour, 1 cup at a time, while kneading for 6-8 minutes in a bread mixer. (May not use entire amount of flour.) Divide into loaves; place into oiled pans. Recipe yields 4-5 loaves. (Also can be made into rolls.) Let rise in a warm place until almost desired bread size and bake for 25 min. in preheated 350° F oven.

—Darla McCoy

Fast and Easy Batter Bread

2½ c. steaming hot tap water (120-130° F)   2 T. sugar
¼ c. oil   2 t. salt
5⅓ c. whole wheat flour   4 t. instant yeast

Put hot water and oil in glass mixing bowl (glass retains heat). Add 4 cups of flour, sugar and salt and beat until combined. Add yeast and beat 3 minutes (by hand 450 strokes). Stir in remaining flour, beating 25 strokes; cover and allow to rise in a warm place until double, about 20 minutes.

Stir batter down, beating 25 strokes; spread evenly in two greased 8x4-inch loaf pans. Smooth tops with floured hand, if desired. Cover; let rise until double, 15-20 minutes. Bake at 375° F for 35 minutes. Remove from pans; cool on rack. Makes 2 loaves.

Oatmeal Batter Bread: Add 1½ cups quick cooking oatmeal and 2½ cups flour in place of 4 cups of the flour in the first addition. Molasses can be substituted for sugar.

Garlic Batter Bread: Add 1 t. garlic powder with sugar and salt.

Onion Batter Bread: Add ¼ c. dried onion and increase water to 2¾ c. + 2 T.

Pinto Bean Bread

1 c. bean puree, made from pinto beans   1 t. salt
1 c. warm water   2 T. gluten flour, sifted
1 T. honey or sugar   2 c. whole wheat flour
1 T. instant yeast   1-1¼ c. white flour
2 t. oil

Puree beans. Combine water and honey in a large bowl; stir in yeast to dissolve. Let stand until foamy. Stir in bean puree, oil, salt and gluten flour. Add whole wheat flour; mix well. Stir in just enough white flour to make a soft dough. Turn out on lightly floured surface; knead until smooth adding a little flour as needed. Put in clean, oiled bowl; let rise until double in size. Punch down and form into loaf. Put into oiled loaf pan; let rise until double. Bake at 350° F for 45-50 minutes until golden brown. Makes 1 loaf.

Bread Rolls

1¾ c. steaming hot tap water (120-130° F)   1 T. instant yeast
½ c. oil   4½-6 c. Favorite Roll Mix, pg. 53
2 T. dried whole egg, sifted

Pour hot tap water into large bowl. Whisk in oil and egg. Stir in 2 cups Favorite Roll Mix. Stir in 1 more cup of Favorite Roll Mix and yeast. Add remaining mix as needed to make a soft dough. Knead dough 5 minutes by hand until smooth (3 minutes in bread mixer, adding mix until dough no longer sticks to side of bowl). Place smooth side down in lightly oiled bowl; turn dough smooth side up. (This oils the top of the dough.) Cover with a damp towel; let rise in a warm place about 40 minutes, until doubled.

Punch dough down. Divide into 16-24 rolls. Form rolls and place in two greased 9-inch round pans or one 9x13-inch pan. Cover; let rise in warm place until about doubled. Preheat oven to 350° F. Bake 20-25 minutes until browned. Makes 16-24 rolls.

Heavenly Cinnamon Rolls

Make the recipe for bread rolls above <u>adding either 1 T. lemon juice with the oil or 1 T. dough enhancer with the Hot Roll Mix</u>. Prepare the following ingredients while dough is rising.

⅓ c. raisins boiled in ½ c. water for 15 min.; cool OR
   ½ c. soaked and chopped dried apples
½ c. sugar or brown sugar, packed
¼ c. powdered butter

1 t. cinnamon
2 T. water
½ c. crushed walnuts (optional)

Combine sugar, butter powder, cinnamon and water together. After dough has risen until doubled, punch down. Roll dough out on a floured surface into a 12x20-inch rectangle. Dot butter/sugar paste over top; then spread over entire surface. Sprinkle with raisins and nuts. Roll dough lengthwise and cut into 12 rolls (about 1½ inches thick). Place cut side down in greased 9x13-inch light-colored pan (dark pans cause rolls to brown more). Cover with towel. Let rise in warm place until almost doubled (about 25-30 minutes—rolls will be dry if allowed to completely fill out the pan when rising). Bake at 350° F for 25 minutes.

Icing:

3 c. powdered sugar
3 T. + 2 t. water

1¼ t. vanilla

Combine ingredients. Icing should be just barely runny; if too thick add ½-1 t. more water. Using the back of a spoon, spread icing on **piping hot** rolls so it can drizzle down inside and cover entire outside of rolls. Enjoy hot or cold. Makes 12 large rolls.

Pita Bread (Pocket Bread)

1½ c. hot tap water (120-130 ° F)
3 T. oil
1 T. dried whole egg, sifted
1 t. salt

½ t. sugar
3-4 c. flour (½ white and ½ whole wheat)
1 T. yeast

Combine water, oil, egg, salt, sugar and 1½ c. flour. Add yeast; stir 1 minute. Add 1½ c. flour to make a soft dough. Knead 5 minutes, adding just enough flour to keep the dough from sticking. Let dough rest 15-30 minutes. Divide into 8 pieces; form into small balls. Roll out into 6-inch circles and place on floured waxed paper. Do not cover, let rest 30-40 minutes. Place circles on ungreased cookie sheet, peeling paper off the dough. Bake 4 minutes at 500° F. Watch carefully—as soon as they are puffed and lightly browned, turn them over and bake for another 1-2 minutes. Remove from oven and cool on cooling rack. Makes 8. Use your imagination for fillings or try the following.

—Charlotte Putman

Turkey Salad Pita Filling

1 (15-oz.) can turkey or 2 (6-oz.) cans tuna, drained
1 T. hydrated dried celery
½ c. hydrated dried apple slices OR
   1 c. raisins

1 t. bottled lemon juice
1 c. salad dressing or mayonnaise
dash of lemon pepper

Mix all ingredients together and fill pocket breads.

—Tresa Hansen

Quick Breads

Whole Wheat Soda Bread

2½ c. whole wheat flour
1 T. dried whole egg, sifted
1 t. baking soda

½ t. salt
1 c. sour milk
2 T. honey

(To make sour milk, put 1 T. lemon juice in bottom of measuring cup and fill to 1 cup with reconstituted dry milk, at room temperature.)

In large bowl, whisk together dry ingredients. Stir honey into sour milk. Pour sour milk mixture into flour mixture; stir just until dry ingredients are moistened. Dough should be sticky. Pour onto greased cookie sheet and shape with hands into a 7-inch round loaf. Bake at 375° for 20 minutes, until golden brown. Remove from cookie sheet and cool on wire rack. Serve warm or cold. Makes 1 loaf.

Fabulous Cornbread

2 c. Super Quick Mix, pg. 53
6 T. cornmeal
⅓ c. sugar

¼ c. powdered butter, sifted
2 T. dried whole egg, sifted
1½ c. reconstituted dry milk or water

Preheat oven to 350° F. Whisk together dry ingredients in a bowl. Add liquid and stir until combined. Pour in greased 8-inch square pan. Bake for 30 minutes. Cut into squares.
Cornmeal Muffins: Spoon batter into greased muffin pans. Bake at 400° F for 15 minutes. Makes 12 muffins (cupcake size).

Magnificent Muffins

3½ c. Super Quick Mix, pg. 53
½ c. sugar

1 T. dried whole egg, sifted
1½ c. water

Whisk together dry ingredients in a bowl. Add water and stir just until ingredients are moistened. Spoon batter into greased muffin pans (they will be very full) and bake at 400° F for 15 minutes until lightly golden brown. Makes 12 muffins (cupcake-size).
Orange Muffins: Decrease sugar to 1 T. and add ½ c. orange-flavored drink powder and 2 t. dried orange peel. Stir gently for 45 strokes before filling muffin pans, (this eliminates the extra leavening reaction created by the drink mix, which makes muffins too airy and dry).
Oatmeal Muffins: Decrease Super Quick Mix to 2¾ c. Add 1 cup quick cooking oatmeal, 1½ T. bran (optional) and increase water to 1⅔ cups.

Biscuits

3¼ c. Super Quick Mix, pg. 53   1¼ c. water

In a bowl, stir Super Quick Mix and water until blended.

Drop Biscuits: Drop dough by tablespoons on greased cookie sheet. Bake at 425° F for 13-15 minutes. Makes 12-14 1½-inch biscuits.

Rolled Biscuits: Pour dough out on generously floured counter (use Super Quick Mix) and generously sprinkle Super Quick Mix on top. Lightly knead dough; about 12 strokes. Pat out to 1-inch thickness. Cut with floured cutter. Place ½-inch apart on greased cookie sheet. Brush tops with reconstituted dry milk. Bake at 425° F for 13-15 minutes. Makes 14 1½-inch biscuits.

Variation: This recipe can be put on top of any casserole and baked. Or make half the rolled biscuit recipe, roll out and use for the top crust of a meat pie.

Basic Crepes

1 c. whole wheat flour   ½ c. dry milk
2 T. dried whole egg, sifted   1¾ c. water
¼ t. salt

Beat all ingredients together until lumps disappear. Fry in hot greased skillet, lightly browning on both sides. Roll each with one of the following fillings inside. Serve warm. Makes about 12.

Filling #1:

1 recipe thick Super Quick White Sauce, pg. 53   1 (10-oz.) can chicken or turkey, chunks
1 (11-oz.) can cream of mushroom or chicken soup   1 (4-oz.) can mushrooms

Using liquid from canned meat and mushrooms, make white sauce. Whisk in soup until there are no lumps; bring to boil. Stir in meat and mushrooms; heat through.

Filling #2: Make Hawaiian Haystack recipe, pg. 94 for filling.

Filling #3: For a sweet crepe, omit salt and add 2 T. sugar to crepes. Fill with pudding and fruit, pie filling or jam. Serve hot or cold. After filled, sprinkle with powdered sugar.

Navajo Fry Bread

4 c. flour (½ whole wheat & ½ white)   1 t. salt
2 T. dry milk   1¾ c. warm water
1 T. baking powder   oil

Mix dry ingredients together. Stir in warm water; add more water if necessary. Knead 3 minutes. Let rest in warm place 45 minutes. Roll 2-inch balls of dough into 8- to 10-inch circles. Heat oil just until it starts to smoke. Fry dough circles 20 seconds on each side until golden brown. Serve in place of rolls or cornbread with bean dishes, soups, or stews. Makes 8, 10-inch breads or tortillas.

—Anna Benally

Corn Tortillas

Masa Harina makes the best corn tortillas but has a short shelf life. This recipe makes tortillas with a great flavor but they will not look like commercial tortillas.

1 c. cornmeal
1 c. white flour
¾ t. salt

¼ c. shortening
⅔ c. hot water

Mix dry ingredients together in a bowl; roughly cut in shortening. Stir in water; knead for 1 minute. Divide dough into 12 equal pieces. Heat heavy skillet, wiped with oil. Roll one dough piece into a 7-inch circle on floured counter. Cook in hot skillet on medium-high heat about 30 seconds on each side. If pan is hot enough, little brown spots will appear on each side as tortillas cook. These go fast—roll tortillas out as you cook them. Makes 12.

Corn Chips: Cut tortillas in quarters and fry in an inch or two of hot oil until crisp. Salt if desired.

Flour Tortillas

1½ c. whole wheat flour
1½ c white flour
1½ t. baking powder

½ t. salt
1 c. <u>very</u> warm water
½ t. heaping, shortening (lard)

Mix dry ingredients together. Add water and mix to make very stiff dough. Knead in shortening to make soft dough. Pinch off 1½-inch balls and roll out very thinly on lightly floured counter. Grill in skillet sprayed lightly with oil. Use for fajitas, burritos or enchiladas. Makes 6-8.

—Anna Benally

Canned Fruit Quick Bread

3 c. flour
2¼ c. whole wheat flour
2¼ c. sugar
3 T. dried whole egg, sifted
3 t. baking soda
1½ t. salt

1½ t. cinnamon
¾ t. ginger (optional)
¾ c. oil
1 (29-oz.) can fruit, drained and chopped, reserving
    1 c. + 2 T. liquid
¼ c. coarsely chopped walnuts (optional)

Grease and flour bottom only of three 8x4-inch loaf pans. In large bowl, combine dry ingredients. Add oil, fruit and reserved fruit liquid. Beat 3 minutes at medium speed. Stir in walnuts. Pour batter into greased and floured pans.

Bake 65 minutes at 325° F or until toothpick inserted in center comes out clean. Cool 5 minutes; remove loaves from pans. Cool on wire rack. Makes 3 loaves.

Banana Nut Bread

2½ c. crushed dried banana chips
2½ c. hot tap water
2¼ c. sugar
¾ c. shortening
3½ t. vanilla
1½ c. whole wheat flour

2 c. white flour
2 T. dried whole egg, sifted
2½ t. baking soda
½ t. salt
1 c. walnuts, chopped

Put banana chips in plastic bag and crush them with a rolling pin. Measure 2½ cups and soak in water with ¼ c. sugar for 40 minutes. Mash bananas with a potato masher; water will thicken while leaving little pieces of banana.

Cream together shortening and remaining 2 cups of sugar. Add vanilla and mashed bananas plus liquid. In separate bowl whisk together dry ingredients. Mix into banana mixture until combined. Stir in walnuts. Bake in 2 greased 8x4-inch loaf pans at 350°F for 1 hour. Remove from pans and cool completely before cutting with serrated knife.

Variation: Substitute other dried fruit for dried bananas.

Salads & Dressings

See Appendix B for helpful information on cooking dried beans/legumes, hydrating dried foods, recipe substitutions, or general information about using food storage items.

Main Dish Salads

Creamy Red Beans and Pasta Salad

4 c. cooked and drained small pasta
3½ c. soaked and cooked dry red beans OR
    2 (15-oz.) cans red beans, drained
½ c. dried carrots

½ c. freeze-dried peas
½ c. bottled Italian dressing
½ c. mayonnaise
2 T. dried parsley

Simmer dried carrots in 1½ cups water for 20 minutes. Add peas and simmer an additional 3-4 minutes. Drain vegetables, combine with pasta and beans and cool. Whisk together dressing, mayonnaise and parsley; pour over salad and toss. Serves 4-5.

White Bean and Bow Tie Salad

12 oz. cooked and drained bow tie or other med. pasta
1¾ c. soaked and cooked dry white beans OR
    1 (15-oz.) can white beans, drained
1 (2-oz.) can sliced black olives, drained

⅔ c. bottled Italian salad dressing
1 t. dried basil
¼ t. garlic powder
2 T. Parmesan cheese

Stir together pasta, beans and olives in a bowl. Combine rest of ingredients except Parmesan cheese; pour over salad. Serve sprinkled with Parmesan cheese. Serves 4.

Southwestern Chicken and Pasta Salad

3 c. cooked and drained elbow macaroni
3½ c. soaked and cooked dry black beans OR
    2 (15-oz.) cans black beans, drained and rinsed
1 (15-oz.) can corn, drained
Dressing:
⅓ c. bottled lime juice
2 T. oil
1 T. honey

1 (10-12-oz.) canned chicken chunks, drained
3 T. hydrated dried green pepper
1 t. dried onion

1 t. cumin
¼ t. hot pepper sauce

Combine salad ingredients and drained green pepper. Blend together dressing ingredients; pour over salad. Toss to coat. Chill 1 hour to blend flavors. Serves 5-6.

Warm Mediterranean White Bean Salad

3½ c. soaked and cooked dry white beans OR
  2 (15-oz.) cans white beans, warmed and drained
2 T. dried green pepper
1 T. dried parsley
1 t. dried onion OR
  2 t. dried chopped chives

3 T. olive oil
1 T. wine vinegar
1 (6-oz.) can tuna, drained (optional)
lettuce (optional)
black olives (optional)

Soak pepper and parsley together in ¼ cup water for 30 minutes; drain. Toss with onion into warm beans. Combine olive oil and vinegar and toss into warm salad. Serve on optional bed of lettuce. Arrange tuna on top of beans, if desired. Garnish with black olives. Serves 4.

Hawaiian Bean Salad

3½ c. soaked and cooked dry red kidney beans, OR
  2 (15-oz.) cans red kidney beans, drained
1¾ c. soaked and cooked dry pinto beans, OR
  1 (15-oz.) can pinto beans, drained
1 (11-oz.) can mandarin oranges, save juice
1 (20-oz.) can pineapple tidbits, drained
1 T. hydrated dried green pepper

1 t. dried onion OR
  2 t. dried chopped chives
½ t. chopped mint (optional)
¼ c. bottled lime juice
2 T. juice from mandarin oranges
2 T. olive oil
¼ t. allspice
¼ t. garlic powder

Put dried green pepper and onion in 1½ T. water to soak for 10-15 minutes, drain. Rinse beans and put in small salad bowl. Add oranges, pineapple, mint (if used), green pepper and onion. Combine rest of ingredients to make a dressing. Pour dressing over salad and toss lightly. Let stand at room temperature 15-30 minutes. Gently toss and serve. Serves 4-5.

Three Bean and Meat Salad

1¾ c. soaked and cooked dry white beans OR
  1 (15-oz.) can white beans, rinsed and drained
1¾ c. soaked and cooked dry kidney beans OR
  1 (15-oz.) can kidney beans, rinsed and drained
1 (15-oz.) can cut green beans, drained
½ c. hydrated dried green pepper

1 t. dried onion
½ t. dried parsley
¼ c. light olive oil
2 T. bottled lemon juice
¼ t. hot pepper sauce
1 can chicken, turkey or tuna, drained
Lettuce (optional)

Combine beans, green pepper, onion and parsley. Whisk together oil, lemon juice and pepper sauce. Pour over salad and toss. Serve salad on lettuce leaf; top with meat. Serves 4.

Mexicali Bean and Rice Salad

6 c. cooked rice
1¾ c. each soaked and cooked dry kidney, pinto and
    black beans OR
    1 (15-oz.) can each kidney, pinto and black
    beans, drained and rinsed

1 (15-oz.) can corn, drained
¼ c. hydrated dried green pepper
½-1 (4-oz.) can diced green chiles

Dressing:
⅓ c. olive oil
¼ c. cider vinegar
1 t. chili powder

½ t. cumin
½ t. garlic salt
½ t. hot pepper sauce

Combine dressing ingredients and set aside. In large bowl, combine rest of ingredients (rice can be warm but not hot). Pour dressing over and toss. Serve immediately or chill 1 hour before serving. Serves 6-8.

Spam and Pasta Salad

10 c. cooked and cooled noodles
1 (15-oz.) can Spam Lite, diced
1 c. pineapple chunks, drained
1 c. cooked and cooled freeze-dried peas

1 (15-oz.) can corn, drained
2 t. dried onion OR
    2 t. dried minced chives
2 T. hydrated dried celery

Dressing:
1 (16-oz.) bottle Kraft coleslaw dressing
3 T. malt or cider vinegar
 2 T. oil

4½ t. sugar
½ t. salt

Combine above salad ingredients in a large bowl. Stir dressing ingredients together and pour over salad. Stir until combined. Chill 2 hours. Serves 6-8.

Chicken Noodle Salad

2 c. cooked and cooled macaroni
1 T. hydrated dried celery
1 t. dried onion
1 (11-oz.) can mandarin oranges, drained

1 (10-oz.) can chicken chunks, drained
1 (20-oz.) can pineapple chunks, drained, reserving
    ¼ c. juice
2 c. seedless grapes (optional)

Dressing:
2 T. brown sugar, packed
¼ c. reserved pineapple juice

2 T. vinegar
1 T. oil

Mix dressing ingredients together.   Toss salad ingredients together. Pour dressing over salad and toss. Chill for 2 hours. Toss salad again and serve. Serves 5-6.

Tuna Noodle Salad

5 c. cooked and drained salad macaroni
1 (6-oz.) can tuna, drained
¾ c. sweet pickles, chopped
2 T. hydrated dried celery
2-3 t. dried onion

vegetables: fresh, cooked, canned (optional)
¾ c. salad dressing (Miracle Whip)
¼ c. reconstituted dry milk
1 t. vinegar OR ¼ c. pickle juice

Shred tuna over noodles. Top with pickles, celery and onion and optional vegetables. Mix salad dressing, milk and vinegar together. Pour over salad; toss to combine. Chill 2 hours before serving. Serves 4-6.

Tropical Chicken Salad

1 (10-12-oz.) can chicken chunks, drained
1 (20-oz.) can pineapple chunks, drained
1 (11-oz.) can mandarin oranges, drained

2 T. hydrated dried celery
⅓ c. mayonnaise
½ t. garlic powder

Combine mayonnaise and garlic powder. Toss with chicken, pineapple and celery. Stir in oranges. Serve in rolls or pita bread. Serves 4.

Side Salads

Rice Salad

3 c. cooked long grain rice
1 (20-oz.) can pineapple chunks, drained
1 (15-oz.) can corn, drained
⅓ c. raisins

2 T. hydrated dried green pepper
2½ t. dried onion OR
    2 T. dried chopped chives

Dressing:
⅓ c. oil
2 T. white vinegar

½ t. sugar
¼ t. dry mustard

Combine dressing ingredients. Toss salad ingredients together in a bowl. Pour dressing over and toss. Chill. Serves 6.

Barley and Corn Salad

1½ c. water
½ c. pearled barley
1 t. chicken bouillon

1 (15-oz.) can corn, drained
2 T. hydrated dried green pepper
1 T. dried parsley

Dressing:
2 T. water
2 T. oil

2 T. bottled lemon juice
¼-½ t. basil

Combine water, barley and bouillon in small saucepan; boil for 45-55 minutes until barley is tender. Meanwhile, soak green pepper; make dressing and set aside. Pour dressing over warm barley. Add corn and drained green pepper; toss. Serve at room temperature or chilled. Serves 6.

Corn Salad

2 (15-oz.) cans corn, drained
2 T. hydrated dried green pepper
Dressing:
1 T. dried parsley
¼ c. bottled lemon juice
2 T. oil
2 t. sugar

1 (2-oz.) can black olives, sliced
2 tomatoes, seeded and chopped (optional)

½ t. cumin
½ t. salt
dash pepper

Gently combine corn, green pepper, olives and tomatoes. In small bowl, whisk together dressing ingredients. Stir into salad and chill 1 hour to blend flavors. Serves 3-4.

Five Bean Salad

⅔ c. oil
⅔ c. vinegar
½ c. sugar
1 t. salt
1 (15-oz.) can lima beans, drained

1 (15 oz.) can, garbanzo beans, drained
1 (15-oz.) can green beans, drained
1 (15-oz.) can yellow beans, drained
1 (15-oz.) can red beans, drained

Combine all ingredients in first column; add beans and marinate overnight or for 2 hours. Serves 10.

—Marlene Rosen

Yummy Potato Salad

3 c. dried diced potatoes
4½ c. water
2-3 lg. sweet pickles, cut into ¼-inch dices
1½ c. mayonnaise

¼ c. water
2 t. prepared mustard
2-3 t. dried onion
½ t. salt

Cook potatoes in 4½ c. water; drain and cool. Put potatoes in a bowl; add pickles. Combine rest of ingredients; stir gently into potatoes and pickles. Chill 2 hours to blend flavors. Serves 5-6.
Fresh potatoes from garden: Replace dried potatoes with 5 cooked medium potatoes, skinned and diced into ½-inch cubes. Omit ¼ c. water and reduce salt to ¼ teaspoon.

Curried Pasta Salad

2 c. any shape cooked and cooled pasta
2½ T. hydrated dried green pepper
1 T. dried onion OR
    2 T. dried chopped chives
Curry Dressing:
¾-1 t. curry powder
2 t. sugar

1 (4-oz.) can sliced mushrooms, drained
¼ c. raisins

¼ c. oil
3 T. vinegar

Combine dressing ingredients. Mix salad ingredients and toss with dressing. Chill. Serves 4.

Italian Pasta Salad

4 c. cooked and cooled any shape pasta bottled Italian Salad Dressing
Any kind of vegetable

    Combine pasta and vegetables; pour dressing over and toss. Chill, stir and serve. Serves 4-6.

Dressings

Vinaigrette Dressing

⅔ c. oil ½ t. dry mustard
¼ c. white vinegar or bottled lemon juice 1½ t. sugar
¼ t. salt

    Combine ingredients in a jar and shake well. Makes 1 cup.

Olive Oil Vinaigrette Dressing

⅔ c. extra light olive oil ½ t. salt
⅓ c. malt vinegar or other ½ t. pepper
2 t. sugar ⅛ t. garlic powder
1 t. dry mustard

    Put all ingredients in a jar and shake well. Pour over salad. Dressing does not require refrigeration. Flavor continues to improve the longer it stands. Makes 1 cup.
—Anna Probert

Balsamic Vinaigrette Dressing

½ c. olive oil 1 T. brown sugar, packed
¼ c. Balsamic vinegar 1 T. Parmesan cheese

    Vigorously stir all ingredients in container. Pour by spoonfuls (so as to incorporate heavier elements) onto salad. Makes ¾ cup.

Fantastic French Dressing

1 (8-oz.) can tomato sauce ½ t. salt
¼ c. oil ¼ t. dry mustard
⅓ c. rice or other vinegar ⅛ t. garlic powder
1 T. brown sugar, packed

    Combine ingredients in jar and shake. Makes 1⅔ cups.
Variation: Reduce vinegar to ¼ cup and add ¼ cup light mayonnaise. Whisk together.

Soups & Stews

Light Soups

Quick Potato Soup

2 c. boiling water
1 t. chicken bouillon
½-¾ c. instant potatoes

1 (12-oz.) can evaporated milk
⅛ t. celery salt
⅛ t. onion salt

Combine ingredients as listed. Heat thoroughly and serve hot or cold. Makes 4 cups.
Variation: Substitute 1 cup broth from drained canned meats for 1 cup water and bouillon.

Potato Soup

3½ c. water
1½ c. dried potato dices
3 T. dried onion
1 T. dried celery
1½ t. chicken bouillon

1 bay leaf
3 c. water
1½ c. Super Quick White Sauce Mix, pg. 53
½ T. dried parsley

Combine ingredients in first column and bay leaf in saucepan and bring to a boil. Simmer 30 minutes. Remove from heat; remove bay leaf and mash potatoes slightly with a potato masher.
Heat the 3 cups water in another saucepan. Whisk in sauce mix and bring to a boil over medium-high heat, stirring constantly. Simmer 1 minute. Combine with potato mixture and add parsley. Stir well, reheat if necessary and serve. Serves 4-5.

Vegetable Cheese Soup

8 c. water
1 c. dried broccoli OR
    combination of dried carrots and celery
2 t. chicken bouillon

¾ c. flour
½ c. powdered butter
1¼ c. water
1 (15-oz.) bottle processed cheese sauce/dip

Combine ingredients in first column in saucepan; bring to boil. Simmer 10 minutes(broccoli); 20 minutes(carrots and celery). Combine flour and butter powder. Add 1¼ cups water; stir until smooth. Remove vegetables from heat; stir in flour mixture. Return to heat. Bring to boil, stirring constantly. Reduce heat; simmer 1 minute. Add cheese; stir just until melted. Makes 12 cups.

Creamy Broccoli Rice Soup

2 c. water
¾ c. uncooked long grain rice

¼ c. dried broccoli
2 (11-oz.) cans condensed cream of chicken soup

Bring water to boil; add rice and broccoli. Simmer, covered, for 20 minutes until rice is done. Add cream of chicken soup plus 2 cans water or half milk and water. Heat and serve. Serves 4-5.

Broccoli Soup OR Tuna Broccoli Soup

4½ c. water
1½ c. dried broccoli
2 T. dried onion
2 t. chicken bouillon
¼ t. dried minced garlic
4 c. reconstituted dry milk

1 c. Super Quick White Sauce Mix, pg. 53
2 (4-oz.) cans mushrooms, undrained
2 (6-oz.) cans tuna in water, undrained
1 T. bottled lemon juice
⅛-¼ t. dried basil (optional)

Combine ingredients in first column, except milk, and simmer 8 minutes. Add milk; stir. Stir in white sauce mix until smooth. Bring soup to boil on medium, stirring continually. STOP HERE FOR BROCCOLI SOUP. Add mushrooms, tuna, lemon juice, and basil. Heat and serve. Serves 4-6.

Legumes

See Appendix B for helpful information on cooking dried beans/legumes.
Mash or puree nutritious diced tomatoes to hide them in recipes when chunks are not desired.

Fabulous Soup Mix Soup

(If your commercial ABC Soup Mix contains no onion, add 2 T. dried onion per cup Soup Mix.)

9 c. boiling water
7-8 t. beef bouillon

1 c. dry legume ABC soup mix

Add bouillon and soup mix to boiling water and simmer, covered for 45 minutes. Serves 6.
Deluxe Soup Variation: Reduce bouillon to 4-5 teaspoons. Add 1 (15-oz.) can diced tomatoes, undrained, and 1 (12-oz.) can of beef chunks, undrained and broken up, the last 15 minutes.
Homemade Legume ABC Soup Mix: Combine 2½ c. (1 lb.) dry lentils, 2½ c. (1 lb.) dry split peas, 2½ c. (12 oz.) alphabet noodles, 1¼ c. long grain rice, and 1¼ c. dried onions. Makes 10 c.

8 Bean Soup

5¼ c. soaked and cooked any combination of
    8 beans (including split peas and lentils)
    OR 3 (15-oz.) cans any beans
6 c. water
½ c. dried diced carrots

¼ c. dried onion
¼ c. dried celery
1 (8-oz.) can tomato sauce
1 t.. cumin
½ t. salt
2 t. bottled lemon juice

In a pot combine all ingredients, except lemon juice; bring to a boil and simmer, covered, 30 minutes. Stir in lemon juice and serve.

Simply Delicious Beans

5¼ c. soaked and cooked any dry legumes OR
    3 (15-oz.) cans any beans, drained
3 c. water
2 T. dried onion
1½ t. beef bouillon
½ t. basil

¼ t. salt (no salt for canned beans)
¼ t. ground cummin
⅛ t. pepper
pinch ginger
pinch garlic powder

Combine all ingredients in a pot; bring to a boil. Simmer, covered, 20-30 minutes. Serves 4-5.
Variation: Add any dried vegetables and required water to hydrate, or fresh vegetables, with the rest of the ingredients.
Gift Idea: A colorful selection of about 2 cups of dried legumes can be layered in a pint canning jar. Write above recipe and cooking instructions on a card and attach to bottle. You can title it "Love 'Bean' Friends with U Soup."

Any Bean Soup with Vegetables

5¼ c. soaked and cooked mixed dry beans OR
    3 (15-oz.) cans any beans, drained
¼ c. each dried carrots, celery and cabbage OR
    ¾ c. dried vegetable stew blend
4¾ c. water

2 T. dried onion
2 t. ham bouillon
pinch garlic powder
pepper to taste

Combine all ingredients in a pot; bring to boil. Cover and simmer 20-30 minutes. Serves 4-5.

Minestrone

3½ c. soaked and cooked mixed dry beans OR
    2 (15-oz.) cans any beans, drained
½ c. dried diced carrots
2 T. dried celery
1 T. dried onion
¾ t. dried minced garlic
½ c. dried cabbage

¼ c. olive oil
1 (6-oz.) cans tomato paste
¼ c. uncooked macaroni or other small pasta
2 T. uncooked rice
1 T. dried parsley
1¼ t. salt (½ t. for canned beans)

Soak carrots, celery, onion and garlic in 1¼ cups water for at least 30 minutes, stirring occasionally. Soak cabbage in separate bowl in 1 cup water for same amount of time. Drain all vegetables, reserving liquid. In non-stick pan, saute carrot mixture in hot olive oil on medium-high heat until lightly browned, about 3 minutes. Add tomato paste stirring quickly. Saute for about 3 minutes to brown paste on bottom of pan, stirring frequently so it does not burn. Add cabbage and brown mixture 1-2 more minutes, stirring constantly. Add 4½ cups of water (including soaking water) and rest of ingredients. Stir to de-glaze pan. Cover and simmer 20 minutes, stirring occasionally. Soup is thick. Serves 5-6.
Note: Browning required for flavor in this recipe goes faster in a pan without a non-stick coating. If using a regular pan, add cabbage with tomato paste and brown only about 3 minutes.

Vegetarian Chili

5¼ c. soaked and cooked mixed dry beans OR
    3 (15-oz.) cans any beans, drained
6 c. water
2 (15-oz.) cans stewed tomatoes, cut up

¼ c. dried onion
2 T. chicken bouillon
½ t. dried minced garlic
½ t. chili powder
pepper to taste

Combine all ingredients in a pot. Bring to a boil; cover and simmer 30 minutes. Serves 6.

—Adapted recipe from Chanalyn Prina

Eureka Kidney Bean Soup

1¾ c. soaked and cooked dry kidney beans OR
    1 (15-oz.) can kidney beans, drained
2 (15-oz.) cans diced tomatoes, undrained
1 (15-oz.) can corn, drained
¼ c. water

1½ T. dried green pepper
1 T. dried onion
½ t. garlic powder
⅛-¼ t. chili powder

In saucepan combine all ingredients; bring to a boil. Simmer 10 minutes, stirring occasionally.
Serves 4.

Lentil Stew

6 c. water
1 c. dry lentils, sorted and rinsed
1 (15-oz.) can diced tomatoes, undrained
1 c. dried diced carrots
½ c. barley
¼ c. dried onion

4 t. chicken bouillon
2 T. brown sugar, packed
1 T. olive oil
¾ t. dried minced garlic
½ t. cumin
¼ t. oregano

Combine all ingredients in saucepan and bring to boil. Reduce heat and simmer, covered, 45-
55 minutes until barley is tender. Serves 6-8.

Lentil Chili

5 c. water
2⅓ c. dry lentils, sorted and rinsed
1½ t. salt
1 (15-oz.) can diced tomatoes

1 pkg. dry onion soup mix
½ t. cumin
¼ t. chili powder

Bring water to boil. Add lentils and salt. Cover and simmer 30 minutes. Add rest of ingredients
and simmer 30 minutes more. Serve as is or over rice, in tortillas, on tostadas, or as a dip.
Serves 4-6.

Lentil Vegetable Soup

8½ c. water
1 c. dry lentils, sorted and rinsed
1 (15-oz.) can diced tomatoes, undrained
½ c. dried diced carrots
½ c. dried potato dices
¼ c. dried onion
2 T. chicken bouillon

1 T. dried celery
1 T. dried green pepper (optional)
½ t. basil
½ t. oregano
½ t. paprika
¼ t. dried minced garlic
1 bay leaf

Combine all ingredients together in a pot. Bring to boil and reduce heat. Simmer, covered, 45-50 minutes. Serves 6-8.

Split Pea Stew

4¼ c. water
1 c. dry split peas
1 (15-oz.) can diced tomatoes, undrained
1 (4-oz.) can sliced mushrooms, undrained
½ c. dried diced carrots

2 T. dried onion
1 T. dried celery
2 t. chicken bouillon
½ t. basil
1 bay leaf

Combine all ingredients in a pot. Bring to boil, then simmer, covered, 45 minutes. Serves 6.

Stretch-A-Can of Chili

Mix 1-2 (15-oz.) cans chili with 1 (15-oz.) can kidney beans, drained. Heat and serve. Serves 2-3.

Legumes and Canned Meats

See Appendix B for helpful information on cooking dried beans/legumes.
Mash or puree nutritious diced tomatoes to hide them in recipes when chunks are not desired.
The following recipes are based on 1-2 tablespoons broth per 12-oz. can of meat. If the canned meats you store have more broth than this, substitute it for water added anywhere in the recipe and reduce bouillon accordingly.

Buckaroo Beans

5¼ c. soaked and cooked dry pinto beans OR
    3 (15-oz.) cans pinto beans, drained
3 c. water
1 (15-oz.) can diced tomatoes, undrained
¼ c. dried onion
2 T. brown sugar, packed
1 t. dried minced garlic

1 t. chili powder
½ t. dry mustard
¼ t. cumin
1 bay leaf
salt to taste (no salt for canned beans)
½ (2-oz.) jar bacon pieces

Combine all ingredients, except bacon, in a pot. Bring to boil; reduce heat and simmer, covered, 30 minutes. Add bacon and serve. Serves 4-5.

Quick Beef Chili and Corn

3½ c. soaked and cooked dry kidney beans OR
    2 (15-oz.) cans kidney beans, drained
1 (15-oz.) can corn, drained
1 (15-oz.) can diced tomatoes, undrained
1 (12-oz.) can beef chunks, undrained and broken up

1½ c. water
1 c. chunky salsa
½ t. cumin
½ t. chili powder (optional)
½ t. sugar (if no sugar in canned corn)

Combine ingredients in pan and simmer 10 minutes, stirring occasionally. Serves 4-5.

Italian Chicken and Bean Soup

5½ c. water
3½ t. chicken bouillon
1½ c. uncooked spiral pasta
2 T. dried green pepper
1 (12-oz.) can chicken chunks, undrained

1¾ c. soaked and cooked dry kidney beans OR
    1 (15-oz.) can kidney beans, drained
1 (15-oz.) can mixed vegetables, drained
¾ t. Italian seasoning

Bring water and bouillon to boil in saucepan and add pasta and green pepper. Simmer, covered, 10 minutes. Add rest of ingredients and heat to boil. Serves 4-5.

Senate Bean Soup

5¼ c. soaked and cooked dry white beans OR
    3 (15-oz.) cans white beans, drained
5½ c. water
3 T. dried onion
1 T. ham bouillon

2 T. dried celery
½ t. dried minced garlic
1 bay leaf
⅔ c. instant potatoes
1 (5-oz.) can chunk ham, broken up
pepper to taste

In large saucepan combine all ingredients except instant potatoes and ham; simmer, covered, 20 minutes. Remove bay leaf. Whisk in potatoes; stir in ham and simmer for 1 minute and serve. Serves 5-6.

Ham 'N Bean Soup (without a ham hock!)

5¼ c. soaked and cooked any dry beans OR
    3 (15-oz.) cans any beans, drained
6 c. water
2 (15-oz.) cans diced tomatoes, undrained
¼ c. dried onions
1 T. ham bouillon

½ t. garlic powder
¼ t. salt (none for canned beans)
¼ t. pepper
¼ t. chili powder
1 (5-oz.) can chunk ham, broken up

Combine all ingredients except ham in a pot. Cover and simmer 30 minutes. Stir ham into soup. Bring to a boil. Serves 6.

White Bean and Turkey Chili

3½ c. soaked and cooked dry white beans OR
    2 (15-oz.) cans white beans, drained
1 (12-oz.) can turkey chunks, undrained
3 c. water
1 (6-oz.) can tomato paste

½ (4-oz.) can diced green chiles, undrained
¼ c. dried onion
2 t. chicken bouillon
1 t. cumin
¼ t. minced garlic
¼ t. sugar

    In a saucepan combine all ingredients. Simmer, covered, 20-30 minutes. Serves 4-5.

Mexican White Bean and Turkey Chowder

3½-5¼ c. soaked and cooked dry white beans OR
    2-3 (15-oz.) cans white beans, drained
4 c. water
1 (12-oz.) can turkey chunks, undrained
1 (12-oz.) can evaporated milk
1 (4-oz.) can diced green chiles
⅓ c. dried onion

4 t. chicken bouillon
¾ t. cumin
¾ t. oregano
¼ t. cinnamon
⅛ t. dried minced garlic
flour to thicken
salt and pepper to taste

    Combine all ingredients except flour, salt and pepper; simmer 10-15 minutes. Remove from heat. Mix flour with a little water until there are no lumps. Stir into chowder; return to heat. Bring to boil; simmer 1 minute, stirring constantly. Salt and pepper if desired. Serves 5-8.   —Patrice Hansen

Chicken, Hominy and White Beans

3½ c. soaked and cooked dry white beans OR
    2 (15-oz.) cans white beans, drained
1 (15-oz.) can hominy, drained
3 c. water
¼ c. dried onion
2 t. chicken bouillon

½ t. cumin
½ t. dried minced garlic
¼ t. coriander
¼ t. oregano
2 T. bottled lime juice
1 t. hot pepper sauce
1 (12-oz.) can chicken chunks, undrained

    Combine all ingredients, except chicken in saucepan; simmer 10-15 minutes. Add chicken; heat through. Serves 5-6.

Lima Bean Soup

5¼ c. soaked and cooked dry lima beans OR
    3 (15-oz.) cans butter beans
6⅔ c. water
⅓ c. dried diced carrots
2 T. dried onion
4 t. ham or chicken bouillon

½ t. dried minced garlic
⅛-¼ t. pepper
⅛-¼ t. hot pepper sauce
salt to taste
½ (2-oz.) jar bacon pieces

    In a pot combine all ingredients except bacon. Simmer, covered, 30 minutes. Stir in bacon and serve. Serves 4-6.

    —Adapted recipe from Randy Mickiewicz

Bean and Bacon Hot Pot

1¼ c. soaked and cooked dry lima beans OR
    2 (15-oz.) cans butter beans, drained
1¼ c. soaked & cooked dry white beans OR
    2 (15-oz.) cans white beans, drained
1 (15-oz.) can diced tomatoes, undrained
1 c. water
¼ c. dried onion
2 T. brown sugar, packed

1 T. dried celery
½ t. ginger
½ t. salt (no salt for canned beans)
¼ t. dried minced garlic
1 T. prepared mustard
1 t. Worcestershire sauce
½ (2-oz.) jar bacon pieces

In saucepan combine all ingredients, except bacon. Simmer, covered, 15 minutes, stirring occasionally. Stir in bacon and serve. Serves 6.

Lentil Bacon Soup

2¼ c. dry lentils, sorted and rinsed
10 c. water
8 t. ham or chicken bouillon
½ c. dried diced carrots
¼ c. dried onion
2 T. dried celery

1 T. dried parsley
½ t. dried minced garlic
½ t. marjoram
½ t. thyme
⅛-¼ t. pepper
½ (2-oz.) jar bacon pieces

Place all ingredients, except bacon, in a pot. Bring to boil and simmer, covered, 45 minutes. Add bacon and serve. Serves 6-8.
Variation: Reduce water to 9 cups and bouillon to 7 teaspoons. Add 1 (15-oz.) can diced tomatoes, undrained.
—Adapted recipe from Annette Harkness

Spicy Hungarian Lentil Stew

7 c. water
1½ c. lentils, sorted and rinsed
⅓ c. dried onion
7 t. chicken bouillon
2 T. tomato paste
2 t. cumin

½-¾ t. cayenne pepper
½ t. dried minced garlic
½ t. paprika
1 large bay leaf
1 (12-oz.) can evaporated milk
2 T. flour

Combine all ingredients except milk and flour in a pot and bring to boil; simmer for 45 minutes. Whisk flour into milk until there are no lumps. Whisk into stew. Return to boil while stirring, simmer 1 minute. Serves 5.

Split Pea Soup

8 c. water
2 c. dry split peas
⅓ c. dried diced carrots
¼ c. dried onion

3½ t. ham bouillon
⅛-¼ t. dried minced garlic
1 bay leaf
1 (5-oz.) can chunk ham, undrained (optional)

Combine all ingredients in pot except ham and bring to boil. Simmer, covered, 1 hour. Break up ham chunks and add to soup last 10 minutes. If desired, mash peas with a potato masher to break them up. Serves 6. (Split peas will break up by themselves if cooked longer.)

Canned Meats

Mash or puree nutritious diced tomatoes to hide them in recipes when chunks are not desired.

The following recipes are based on 1-2 tablespoons broth per 12-oz. can of meat. If the canned meats you store have more broth than this, substitute it for water added anywhere in the recipe and reduce bouillon accordingly.

Beef Barley Stew

1 (12-oz.) can beef chunks
7 c. water
¾ c. dried carrots
3 T. dried onion
3 T. dried celery
2 T. dried red or green pepper

2 T. beef bouillon
2 T. dried minced parsley
½ t. basil
⅛ t. pepper
1 bay leaf
¾ c. pearled barley

Combine all ingredients except barley in large pot and bring to a boil. Add barley and simmer, covered, for 45-55 minutes until barley is tender. Remove bay leaf before serving. Serves 4-6.

—Adapted recipe from Annette Harkness

Beef Stew

9¼ c. water
1½ c. dried potato dices
¾ c. dried diced carrots
2 T. dried onion
8 t. beef bouillon
1 t. Worcestershire sauce

1 bay leaf
1 (12-oz.) can beef chunks, broken up
1 c. freeze-dried peas
1 c. water
3 T. cornstarch

Combine ingredients in first column and bay leaf together in saucepan and bring to boil. Simmer 20 minutes. Add roast beef and peas; simmer 5 minutes. To 1 cup water add cornstarch and stir until lumps are gone. Remove stew from heat and remove bay leaf. Stir in cornstarch mixture. Return to heat and bring to boil, stirring constantly. Simmer 1 minute. Serves 5-6.

Beef Stew with Commercial Brown Gravy Mix:

Make above recipe for Beef Stew using only 4½ t. bouillon and omit Worcestershire sauce. To the last 1 cup water at the end, add 1 package Brown Gravy Mix and 2 tablespoons cornstarch instead of 3.

Southwestern Chicken or Turkey Barley Soup

6 c. water
⅓ c. pearled barley
2 T. dried onion
2 t. chicken bouillon
1 (15-oz.) can diced tomatoes, undrained
1 (15-oz.) can tomato sauce

1 (15-oz.) can corn, drained
1 (4-oz.) can diced green chiles
1 T. chili powder
½ t. cumin powder
⅛ t. garlic powder
1 (10-oz.) can chicken or turkey chunks

Bring first 4 ingredients to boil, then simmer, covered, until barley is tender about 45-55 minutes. Add the rest of ingredients, except chicken or turkey, and simmer 10 minutes until flavors are blended. Add meat and heat through. Serves 6-8.

Chicken Corn Soup

6 c. water
4 t. chicken bouillon
½ c. dried diced carrots
1 T. dried onion
1 T. dried celery
½ t. dried minced garlic

1 (15-oz.) can corn, undrained
2 t. dried parsley
1 c. uncooked noodles, any shape
1 (10-oz.) can chicken chunks with broth, broken up
½ t. sugar (if no sugar in canned corn)
pepper (optional)

Combine ingredients in first column, corn and parsley. Simmer, covered, 15 minutes. Add noodles and simmer 10 minutes. Stir in chicken. Heat through. Serves 4-5.
Garden Vegetable Variation: Omit dried celery and carrots and add 2 peeled and sliced carrots, 1 sliced zucchini and 1 sliced stalk of celery, all sauteed in a little olive oil for 2 minutes. With noodles add 1½ cups broccoli cut into bite size pieces.

Creamy Chicken and Rice Soup

8½ c. water
¾ c. uncooked long grain rice
2 T. chicken bouillon
½ c. dried diced carrots
3 T. dried onion
3 T. dried celery

½ t. dried minced garlic
1 (12 oz.) can evaporated milk
1 (10-12 oz.) can chicken chunks, broken up
3 T. dried parsley
salt and pepper to taste

In a pot, bring water to boil. Add rest of ingredients in first column, garlic and evaporated milk. Simmer 20 minutes, until rice and vegetables are cooked. Stir in chicken, parsley, salt and pepper. Serves 6-8.

Chicken 'N Dumplings

1 (50-oz.) can Whole Chicken
4¾ c. water
1 (4-oz.) can sliced mushrooms, undrained
1 c. dried diced carrots
2 T. dried celery
2 T. dried onion

1 t. chicken bouillon
¼ t. poultry seasoning
1 bay leaf
1 c. freeze-dried peas
½ c. water
5 T. flour

Skim fat off top of opened whole chicken can. Drain broth into a pot. Remove skin and bones from chicken and cut meat into chunks; set aside. Add rest of ingredients except peas, ½ cup water and flour to the broth; simmer, covered, 20 minutes. Meanwhile, in a bowl, whisk together dry ingredients for dumplings below.

Mix the flour in ½ cup water until there are no lumps. Remove pot from heat, remove bay leaf and stir in flour mixture. Return to heat; stir until boiling and thickened. Add chicken and peas; bring to boil. Reduce heat.

Add milk and water to dumpling dry ingredients; stir until combined (dough should be stiff). Drop by heaped tablespoons (about 6-8) onto simmering stew. Cover; simmer 10 minutes without lifting lid. Serve at once. Serves 6-8.

Dumplings:
1 c. flour
1 T. dried whole egg, sifted
1 T. dried parsley

2½ t. baking powder
½ t. salt
½ c. reconstituted dry milk
2 T. water

Variation: In place of canned chicken, substitute 1 (12.5-oz.) can chicken chunks. Increase water to 7½ cups and bouillon to 3¾ teaspoons.

Reckless Ramen

2-3 c. any dried vegetables (including broccoli)
4-6 c. water

2-3 pkg. chicken or shrimp flavor ramen noodles
1 (6-10-oz.) can chicken chunks or
    broken shrimp, drained

Cook vegetables in water 10 minutes. Drain liquid into a large measuring cup; add enough additional water to make required liquid for noodles. Add water to vegetables and bring to boil. Add noodles and cook as directed on package. Stir in seasoning packets and meat. Heat and serve. Serves 4-6.

Salmon Chowder

4½ c. water
2 c. dried potato dices
2 T. dried onion

½ c. freeze-dried peas
½ (5-oz.) bottle processed sharp cheese spread
1 (12-oz.) can evaporated milk
1 (15-oz.) can salmon, undrained

Cook potatoes and onions in water and liquid from salmon for 5 minutes. Add dried peas; cook for another 5 minutes. Remove bones from salmon and break meat into chunks. Stir cheese into potato mixture until melted. Add milk and salmon. Heat through; do not boil. Serves 4-5.

New England Clam Chowder

2 (6½-oz.) cans minced clams
1½ c. dried potato dices
¼ c. dried onion
1 T. dried celery
7-7½ c. water, divided

⅔ c. instant dry milk
1½ c. Super Quick White Sauce Mix, pg. 53
¼ t. sugar
salt and pepper to taste

Drain clams into measuring cup and add enough water to make 4 cups. Pour in pot; add vegetables. Bring to boil, reduce heat and simmer, covered, 10 minutes. The last few minutes vegetables are cooking, heat another 4 cups of water in another saucepan until warm. Whisk in dry milk, white sauce mix and sugar. Heat, stirring constantly, until boiling. Simmer 1 minute.

When vegetables have cooked 10 minutes they should have about 1½ cups water left in pan. If not, add water. Add white sauce, clams, sugar, salt and pepper. Heat and serve. Serves 6.

Corn Chowder

5¼ c. water
1 c. dried diced potatoes
¼ c. dried onion
½ t. salt

⅓ c. instant dry milk
¾ c. Super Quick White Sauce Mix, pg. 53
1 (15-oz.) can cream-style corn
dash pepper
½ (2-oz.) jar bacon pieces

Add potatoes, onion and salt to 3¼ c. *water* in a pot and bring to boil. Reduce heat and simmer, covered, 10 minutes. The last few minutes of cooking time, heat remaining 2 cups water in another saucepan until warm. Whisk in dry milk and white sauce mix. Heat until boiling, stirring constantly. Simmer 1 minute.

When vegetables have cooked 10 minutes, they should have about 1 cup liquid left in pan. If not, add water. Stir white sauce into cooked vegetables with cream-style corn, bacon and pepper. Heat through and serve. Serves 6.

Main Dishes

Light Dishes

Rich Italian Mushroom Sauce and Pasta

2 (4-oz.) cans sliced mushrooms, undrained
1 t. dried minced garlic
½ t. chicken bouillon
½ t. thyme

2 (12-oz.) cans evaporated milk
¼ c. flour
½ t. salt
6 c. cooked ribbon noodles

Stir together a little evaporated milk and flour until lumps are gone. Stir in remaining milk and add rest of ingredients. Bring to boil over medium heat, stirring constantly; simmer 1 minute. Serve over noodles. Serves 4-6.

Scalloped Potatoes

3½ c. water
2 c. dried potato dices
3 T. dried onion
½ t. chicken bouillon

1¼ c. warm water
1 c. Super Quick White Sauce Mix, pg. 53
1 (15-oz.) can Spam Lite, diced OR
    2 (5-oz.) cans chunk ham, broken up

Place potatoes, onion and bouillon in 3½ c. water and simmer 20 minutes. In separate saucepan, whisk white sauce mix into 1¼ c. warm water. Bring to boil and simmer for 1 minute. Drain any remaining liquid from potatoes. Stir white sauce into potato mixture. Add a little more water if too thick. Stir in meat. Serves 4-6.
Optional: Omit meat and serve as a side dish.
Variation: Omit chicken bouillon in cooking. Use only ½ cup water and add ½ cup white sauce mix. Make into sauce. Add 1 (10-oz.) can cream of chicken or mushroom soup to sauce and combine well. Stir into potatoes.

Fried Rice

2 T. dried whole egg + ¼ c. water
⅔ c. dried diced carrots + 1⅓ c. water
⅔ c. freeze-dried peas + ⅔ c. water + ⅛ t. sugar
2 T. dried onion + 3 T. water
3 T. oil

5 c. long grain rice, cooked
2 t. dried onion, not hydrated
½ (2-oz.) jar bacon pieces
soy sauce

Hydrate peas and onions in separate cups with their own water while proceeding with this recipe. Hydrate carrots in water in a saucepan; simmer for 5 minutes.
Mix eggs in their water until there are no lumps. In non-stick frying pan scramble eggs in a little oil. Remove from pan and dice. Saute drained onion in oil on medium-high heat for 2 minutes, stirring often. Add drained carrots and cook further 3-4 minutes while stirring. Add drained peas and cook 2-3 minutes more. Quickly stir in rice, eggs and bacon. When heated through season with soy sauce to taste. Stir in 2 teaspoons dried onion and serve immediately. Serves 4-6.

80

Fettuccine Carbonara

cooked Fettuccine noodles
2½ c. water
1 c. Super Quick White Sauce Mix, pg. 53

½ c. Parmesan cheese
½ (2-oz.) jar bacon pieces

Combine water, white sauce mix, and Parmesan cheese in saucepan. Bring to boil, whisking constantly; simmer 1 minute. Add bacon. Serve immediately over hot noodles. Serves 4-6.
Variation: Add cooked peas.
Salmon Variation: Make sauce above using half the water, sauce mix and Parmesan. Add 1 (15-oz.) can green beans, drained and ½ t. tarragon; heat to boiling. Drain 1 (15-oz.) can salmon; remove bones and break up. Stir lightly into sauce; heat and serve over cooked bow tie pasta. Serves 4-5.

Legumes

See Appendix B for helpful information on cooking dried beans/legumes.
Mash or puree nutritious diced tomatoes to hide them in recipes when chunks are not desired.

Mexican Bean Sauce with Fettuccine

1¾ c. soaked and cooked any dry beans OR
    1 (15-oz.) can any beans, drained
1 (15-oz.) can stewed tomatoes, undrained, cut up
1 (15-oz.) can diced tomatoes, undrained
½ (4-oz.) can chopped green chiles
¼ c. dried onion

¼ t. sugar
¼ t. dried minced garlic
¼ t. chili powder
¼ t. oregano
½ t. dried cilantro (optional)
4 c. hot cooked fettuccine

Combine all ingredients except beans in saucepan and simmer 15 minutes, stirring occasionally. Mash beans slightly, and stir into tomato mixture. Bring to boil and serve over hot cooked fettuccine. Serves 4.

Cheesy Beans and Rice

1 c. long grain rice
1 (15-oz.) can corn, reserving liquid
1¾ c. soaked and cooked dry kidney beans OR
    1 (15-oz.) can kidney beans, drained
1 (4-oz.) can sliced mushrooms, reserving liquid

½-1 (4-oz.) can diced green chiles
1 T. dried onion
2 c. water (include liquid from corn and mushrooms)
2 (8-oz.) cans tomato sauce
1 t. garlic powder
1 (5 oz.) bottle processed sharp cheese spread

Layer first 6 ingredients in the order they're listed in a greased 2-qt. casserole. Combine water, tomato sauce and garlic powder in saucepan and bring to boil. Pour tomato mixture over top of casserole. Dot with cheese. Bake, uncovered, at 400° F for 40 minutes. Serves 6-8.
Stove Top Method: Combine all ingredients except cheese in saucepan and bring to boil. Simmer 20 minutes. Add cheese and stir until melted.
Option: In place of processed cheese spread, hydrate 1 c. of freeze-dried cheese in ½ c. lukewarm water while preparing the recipe. Sprinkle hydrated cheese over top of dish before baking.

Bean and Lentil Rice Pilaf

2¼ c. water
2 T. dried onion
2 T. olive oil
2 t. beef bouillon
¼ c. dry lentils, sorted and rinsed

1¾ c. soaked and cooked dry kidney beans OR
    1 (15-oz) can kidney beans, drained
1 (15-oz.) can corn, drained
1 c. uncooked long grain rice
1 c. salsa
1 t. chili powder

In a saucepan combine ingredients in first column and bring to a boil. Reduce heat; cover and simmer 15 minutes. Stir in remaining ingredients and bring to a boil. Reduce heat; cover and simmer 20-25 minutes longer until lentils and rice are tender. Serves 6.

—Adapted recipe from Tatiana Allen

Pinto Bean Wraps

1¾ c. soaked and cooked dry pinto beans OR
    1 (15-oz.) can pinto beans, drained
½ c. salsa
1 recipe Spanish Rice, pg. 98
10 flour tortillas, pg. 60

Optional:
bottled processed sharp cheese spread
shredded lettuce
chopped tomatoes

Add pinto beans and salsa to hot Spanish Rice. Spread warmed tortillas with cheese spread, if used, and fill with pinto bean mixture. Top with lettuce and tomatoes if available. Fills 10 tortillas.

Plain Pinto Beans with Pickle Relish

Heat a can of plain pinto beans. Serve with pickle relish on the side.

Red Beans and Rice
Adapted from a gourmet New Orleans recipe

5¼ c. soaked and cooked dry red beans OR
    3 (15-oz.) cans red beans, drained
2 c. water
½ c. dried onion
¼ c. dried green pepper
1 T. dried parsley
1 t. garlic powder
1 t. salt (¼ t. salt for canned beans)

2 bay leaves
½ t. thyme
¼-½ t. pepper
⅛ t. cayenne
⅛ t. basil
1 (5-oz.) can chunk ham, broken up (optional)
½ t. Liquid Smoke

Combine all ingredients, except ham and Liquid Smoke, in a pot and bring to boil. Reduce heat and simmer, covered, 30 minutes. Most of the liquid should be evaporated.

Add chunk ham and cook 5 minutes more. Remove from heat and stir in liquid smoke. Serve over hot cooked rice. Serves 6.

—Adapted recipe from Laurel Rapp

Puerto Rican Black Beans and Rice

3½ c. soaked and cooked dry black beans OR
    2 (15-oz.) cans black beans, undrained
¾ c. water (½ c. for canned beans)
1 T. dried green pepper
1 T. dried onion
2 T. ketchup
½ T. olive oil

1 t. oregano
½ t. black pepper
½ t. sugar
¼ t. salt (none for canned beans)
¼ t. garlic powder
hot cooked rice

Put beans and all other ingredients together in a pot; bring to boil. Reduce heat and simmer, uncovered, 20 minutes. Serve over hot rice. Serves 4-5.

Stretch-A-Can of Baked Beans

1 (28-oz.) can baked beans
2 (15-oz.) cans kidney beans, drained
1 (15-oz.) can butter beans, drained
1 (8-oz.) can tomato sauce

¼ c. ketchup
2 T. dried onion
2 T. brown sugar, packed
dash pepper

Combine and pour into greased 1½-quart baking dish. Bake at 425° F for 25-30 minutes. Serves 4-5.

Stove Top Method: Combine ingredients in saucepan, substituting 1½ teaspoons onion powder for onion. Heat through on medium heat, stirring often; reduce heat and simmer 5 minutes.

Zippy-Quick Baked Beans

1 (15-oz.) can baked beans
1 (15-oz.) can kidney beans, drained
½ c. thick 'n chunky salsa

½ t. onion powder
¼ t. prepared mustard (optional)

Combine in saucepan and heat through on low heat stirring often. Serves 3-4.

Fiesta Refried Beans

1 (15-oz.) can refried beans
1 c. salsa
½ -1 (4-oz.) can diced green chiles

1 (5-oz.) bottle processed sharp cheese spread
2 t. dried onion
1 (2-oz.) can sliced black olives, drained

In a bowl combine beans, salsa and chiles. Spread in a 2 qt. shallow baking dish. Dot with cheese and sprinkle with onion. Bake at 400° F for 15 minutes. Garnish with olives. Serve with chips or spread on broken pieces of flour tortilla. Makes 3½ cups.

Option: In place of processed cheese spread, hydrate 1 c. of freeze-dried cheese in ½ c. lukewarm water while preparing the recipe. Sprinkle hydrated cheese over top of dish before baking.

Savory Indian Lentils

3¼ c. water
1 c. dry lentils, sorted and rinsed, OR split peas
¼ c. dried onion
1 t. salt
1 t. turmeric

1 t. cumin
½ t. dried minced garlic
¼ t. cardamon
¼ t. sugar
bottled lime juice (optional)

Combine all ingredients in 2-quart saucepan and simmer, covered, 45 minutes. Remove lid and continue simmering, stirring frequently, 20 minutes until mixture is the consistency of refried beans. Serve sprinkled with lime juice. Serves 5. Great with Corn Fritters, pg. 97.

—Carolyn Bargeron

Santa Fe Lentils

1 c. dry lentils, sorted and rinsed
2 c. water
1 (4-oz.) can chopped green chiles
2 T. dried onion

2 t. chicken bouillon
½ t. garlic powder
¼ t. cumin
¼ t. oregano

Combine all ingredients in medium saucepan and heat to boiling. Reduce heat and simmer, covered, 45 minutes. Mash lentils with a potato masher to break them up. Makes 3½ cups. Serve as follows:

Soft Shell Taco: Spread a little bit of bottled processed sharp cheese spread down the middle of flour tortillas, pg. 61. Top with Santa Fe Lentils, then salsa or fresh chopped tomatoes and shredded lettuce.

Tostadas: Spread a little bit of bottled processed cheese spread on fried corn or flour tortillas. Spread Santa Fe Lentils over cheese. Top with salsa or chopped fresh tomatoes and lettuce.

Dip: Combine Santa Fe Lentils with ½ c. salsa and a little bottled processed sharp cheese spread. Use as dip for tortillas, crackers or fresh vegetables.

Legumes and Canned Meats

See Appendix B for helpful information on cooking dried beans/legumes.

Mash or puree nutritious diced tomatoes to hide them in recipes when chunks are not desired.

The following recipes are based on 1-2 tablespoons broth per 12-oz. can of meat. If the canned meats you store have more broth than this, substitute it for water added anywhere in the recipe and reduce bouillon accordingly.

Pork 'N Beans Baked Beans

3 (15-oz.) cans Pork 'N Beans
2 T. dried onion
3 T. brown sugar, packed

1½ T. Worcestershire sauce
1½ t. prepared mustard
½ (2-oz.) jar bacon pieces

Combine all ingredients and pour into greased 1½-quart casserole. Bake, uncovered, at 400° F for 40 min. Serves 5-6.

Darker, Sweeter Variation: Eliminate Worcestershire sauce. Increase brown sugar to ½ cup and add 3 tablespoons molasses and 2 tablespoons ketchup.

Discount brands of pork 'n beans have a little more liquid which can make the above recipe runny. Drain some of the liquid before combining into the recipe.

Spamtastic Pork 'N Beans

2 (15-oz.) cans Pork 'N Beans
¼ c. ketchup
1 T. dried onion
¼ t. dried minced garlic

1 (12-oz.) can Spam Lite
1 (20-oz.) can pineapple chunks
¼ c. brown sugar, packed

Combine beans with ingredients in first column. Pour into greased 8x12-inch casserole. Slice Spam into 11 slices and lay on top of beans, covering them. Drain pineapple, reserving 1 tablespoon liquid. Sprinkle pineapple over top of Spam. Combine reserved liquid with brown sugar and drizzle over top of pineapple and Spam. Bake at 400° F for 40 min. Serves 6.

Discount brands of pork 'n beans have a little more liquid which can make the above recipe runny. Drain some of the liquid before combining into the recipe.

Bean or Beef Spaghetti

Add a can of drained, mashed beans, or a can of roast beef, broken up, to a jar of your favorite spaghetti sauce. Heat and serve over hot cooked spaghetti. Top with Parmesan cheese.

Navajo Tacos

1 recipe Navajo Fry Bread, pg. 59
1-2 (15-oz.) cans chili

shredded lettuce (optional)
chopped fresh tomatoes (optional)

Heat chili serve over bread. Top with lettuce and tomatoes.

Chili on Spaghetti

Great way to stretch a can of chili!

1 (15-oz.) can chili
1 (15-oz.) can diced tomatoes, undrained
1 (4-oz.) can sliced mushrooms, drained

½-1 (5-oz.) bottle processed sharp cheese spread
Cooked spaghetti for 4-5

Combine all ingredients except spaghetti in saucepan and heat until cheese is melted. Serve over spaghetti. Serves 4-5.

Variation: Tomatoes can be eliminated from this recipe for a very rich and delicious option.

Beef or Chicken and Bean Enchiladas

Sauce: 2 T. oil
3 T. flour
2 (8-oz.) cans tomato sauce
1½ c. water (including broth
from canned meat)

2 T. dried onion
½ t. - 2 T. chili powder
½ t. sugar
½ t. vinegar
¼ t. garlic powder

Filling: 1 (12-oz.) can beef or chicken chunks,
drained and broken up
3½ c. cooked any beans OR
2 (15-oz.) cans any beans, drained

1 (4-oz.) can diced green chiles

1 t. onion powder

12 corn tortillas, pg. 60
1 (8-oz.) bottle processed sharp cheese spread

In saucepan, combine oil and flour until there are no lumps. Add rest of sauce ingredients and bring to boil while stirring. Reduce heat; simmer 5 minutes, stirring occasionally. Cool while making tortillas.

In a bowl combine beef, beans and chilies. Spread ⅓ cup sauce over bottom of lightly greased 9x13-inch baking dish. Fill tortillas with ⅓ c. meat mixture and 1 tablespoon of sauce. Roll and place seam side down in pan. Cover enchiladas with remaining sauce. Dot with processed cheese spread and bake, uncovered, at 350° F for 35 minutes.   —Adapted recipe from Darla McCoy

Option: In place of processed sharp cheese spread, hydrate 1 c. of freeze-dried cheese in ½ c. lukewarm water while preparing the recipe. Sprinkle hydrated cheese over top of dish before baking. Substitute garlic salt for garlic powder in the sauce.

Pinto Beef Tamale Pie

1¼ c. cornmeal	1 (4-oz.) can diced green chiles
½ t. salt	¼ c. water
1 (12-oz.) can evaporated milk	½ t. onion powder
1 c. water	½ t. garlic powder
1 (12-oz.) can beef chunks, undrained	½ t. cumin
3½ c. cooked pinto beans OR	¼ t. sugar
2 (15-oz.) cans pinto beans, drained	¼-½ t. chili powder

Combine first four ingredients in small saucepan. Cook on medium heat. Stir until bubbling; continue stirring until <u>very</u> thick, 2-3 more minutes. Save ½ cup cornmeal mixture; cover with plastic wrap. Put rest of mixture in a lump in bottom of greased 10-inch pie plate. Allow to cool 2-3 minutes. Using a slightly wet hand, press dough to cover bottom and sides of plate. Bake in 425° F oven for 10 minutes.

While crust is baking, pour beef into medium saucepan and break up. Add rest of ingredients and bring to a boil. Simmer, covered, 5 minutes, stirring often. Spread pinto beef mixture over baked cornmeal. On a piece of waxed paper flatten reserved cornmeal into a 8-inch round. Place on center of bean filling. Bake pie for further 15 minutes and serve. Serves 6.

Variations: Pinto beef filling can also be served in tortillas, on tostadas or over rice.

Lasagne

12 cooked lasagne pieces, drained and held in cold water	2½ c. water
1 (28-oz.) jar spaghetti sauce	1¾ c. Super Quick White Sauce Mix, pg. 53
1 (15-oz.) can any beans, drained & mashed OR	1 bay leaf
1 (12-oz.) can beef chunks, drained	⅓ c. Parmesan cheese

Combine spaghetti sauce and beans or beef in saucepan and heat. In another saucepan, whisk white sauce mix into 2½ cups of warm water. Add bay leaf and stir until sauce comes to a boil. Remove bay leaf and whisk in Parmesan cheese. Pour into a measuring cup with a pour spout and cover with plastic wrap that touches the surface of the sauce to prevent lumps.

Spread a little spaghetti sauce on bottom of 9x13-inch baking pan. Top with noodles and spread with a ⅓ of the spaghetti sauce. Evenly drizzle ⅔ cup of white sauce over the top of the spaghetti sauce. Repeat these layers two more times; top with fourth layer of noodles and spread last of white sauce mix over entire surface of noodles. Sprinkle with additional Parmesan cheese. Bake at 375° F for 35 minutes until surface is lightly browned. Serve immediately, sliding lasagne off serving spatula with a knife. Serves 6-8.

Canned Meats

Mash or puree nutritious diced tomatoes to hide them in recipes when chunks are not desired.
The following recipes are based on 1-2 tablespoons broth per 12-oz. can of meat. If the canned meats you store have more broth than this, substitute it for water added anywhere in the recipe and reduce bouillon accordingly.

Creamed Meat on Rice

1 double recipe bechamel sauce (See Super
    Quick White Sauce Mix, pg. 53)
1 t. dried parsley

2 (6-oz.) cans tuna, drained OR
    other canned meat, drained
rice, hot cooked

Stir parsley into bechamel sauce. Add meat, cut into smaller chunks if needed, to sauce. Heat through and serve over hot rice. Serves 4-5.

Meat and Gravy on Mashed Potatoes

2 c. water
2 t. beef bouillon
½ t. Kitchen Bouquet
¼ t. onion powder

2½ T. cornstarch
1 (12-oz.) can beef chunks, broken up
instant mashed potatoes, cooked

Combine water, bouillon, Kitchen Bouquet and onion powder in saucepan. Stir in cornstarch until there are no lumps. Bring to boil stirring until thickened. Add undrained can roast beef and stir until it boils again. Serve beef and gravy over generous serving of mashed potatoes. May also be served over rice or noodles. Serves 4-6.

Variation: Substitute canned chicken or turkey; eliminate Kitchen Bouquet and use chicken bouillon instead of beef.

Meat and Gravy with Commercial Gravy Mix:

1 can meat, undrained

1 pkg. commercial dry gravy mix

Measure liquid from can and combine with water to equal liquid called for on gravy package directions. In sauce pan, combine this liquid, meat, and gravy mix; boil until thickened.

Croquettes (Chicken, Turkey, Ham or Beef)

1⅓ c. warm water (include liquid from
    canned meat)
1½ c. Super Quick White Sauce Mix, pg. 53
1 t. dried onion.
1 (12-oz.) can meat, broken up

1 t. dried parsley
2 T. dried whole egg, sifted
6 T. water
1 c. dry bread crumbs
oil

In saucepan combine white sauce mix, onion and water. On medium-high heat, stir constantly until mixture is <u>very</u> thick and bubbling. Reduce heat; cook 1 minute. Remove from heat; stir in meat and parsley. Spread mixture in ungreased 8-inch square pan. Cover and chill 2 hours.

In small bowl, whisk egg into 6 tablespoons of water until there are no lumps. Cut meat mixture into 12 equal parts. Shape each into a 1x2-inch log shape. (This mixture will be sticky so you have to work quickly.) Using forks, dip each ball immediately into egg mixture; then roll in bread crumbs until completely coated. Cover croquettes; chill 30 minutes.

Heat 3-4 inches of oil in saucepan. Fry croquettes until light brown. Drain. Keep very warm until serving time. Serves 4.

Variation: These can also be made with a (15-oz.) can salmon or 2 (6-oz.) cans tuna. Add 1 teaspoon bottled lemon juice with fish to the white sauce, if desired.

Country Meat Pie

1 double crust 10-inch pie crust, pg. 103
½ c. dried carrots
1 (15-oz.) can sliced potatoes, drained OR
    ¾ c. dried potato dices
½ c. freeze-dried peas

2 pkg. commercial dry gravy mix
1½ t. flour
1 (12-oz.) can beef, turkey or chicken chunks,
    broken up

While preparing pie crust, cook dried vegetables together in saucepan for 10 minutes in 1 cup water for each dried vegetable used (add peas last 2-3 minutes of cooking). Roll out half of the crust and place in bottom of 10-inch pie plate.

Combine gravy mix and flour in saucepan. Using broth from canned meat and liquid from cooked vegetables, cook gravy according to package directions. Add meat and vegetables; pour mixture into pie. Roll out rest of pie crust and place on top of pie. Crimp edges, cut a few holes in top crust and bake at 400° F for 25-30 minutes. Cool 5 minutes before serving.

Homemade Gravy:

2 c. water (including broth from canned meat)
3 T. cornstarch
2 t. beef bouillon

¼ t. onion powder
½ t. Kitchen Bouquet for beef gravy

Combine ingredients in saucepan; stir until cornstarch has no lumps. Bring to boil, stirring constantly. Simmer 1 minute, add vegetables and pour into pie.

Tamales

2¼ c. cornmeal
2 t. chili powder
1 t. chicken bouillon
½ t. salt

½ c. shortening
¾ c. hot water
1 (15-oz.) can chili without beans
10 corn husks

Mix first 6 ingredients together; knead until well combined. Soften husks in warm water. Lay husks out; divide dough evenly between them. Spread dough out into circles ½-inch smaller than long sides of the husks. Put rounded tablespoon of chili in middle of each. Using the husk to prevent it from sticking to your hands, fold dough over top of filling. Fold the sides of the husks over the filled tamale, overlapping them 3-4 inches. Tie ends closed or tuck them under tamales. Stack tamales 4 high in steamer; steam 45 minutes. Makes 10 tamales.   —Anna Benally

Barbecue Beef Casserole

6 c. uncooked ziti or rotini pasta
2 (15-oz.) cans diced tomatoes, drained
1 (12-oz.) can beef chunks, broken up
1 (6-oz.) can tomato paste
¼ c. ketchup
2 T. dried green pepper
2 T. brown sugar, packed
1 T. dried onion

1 T. vinegar
1 T. Worcestershire sauce
½ t. salt
¼ t. allspice
¼ t. hot pepper sauce
⅛ t. pepper
1 (5 oz.) bottle processed sharp cheese spread

Cook pasta; drain. Meanwhile, combine rest of ingredients except cheese in a saucepan and simmer, covered, 10 minutes. Stir in pasta. Spread in greased 9x13-inch pan. Dot with cheese and bake, uncovered, at 350° F for about 15 minutes until hot and cheese melts. Serves 8.
Stove Top Method: Combine casserole in large fry pan. Heat; dot with cheese. Cover and allow to stand for a few minutes.
Option: In place of processed cheese spread, hydrate 1 c. of freeze-dried cheese in ½ c. lukewarm water while preparing the recipe. Sprinkle hydrated cheese over top of dish before baking.

Swiss Steak with Parsley Potato Rounds

2 c. water
1 pkg. commercial dry brown gravy mix
½ c. dried diced carrots
2 T. dried onion
1 (15-oz.) can diced tomatoes, undrained
¼ t. onion powder
dash pepper

1 (12-oz.) can beef chunks, broken up
1½ c. water
1½ c. reconstituted dry milk
1 T. powdered butter
1½ c. instant potatoes
1½ T. dried parsley

Stir gravy mix into 2 cups water and add rest of ingredients in first column; bring to boil while stirring. Reduce heat; simmer 30 minutes, stirring occasionally. Add beef; bring to boil and simmer while fixing potatoes. Combine water and milk in another saucepan. Add butter powder; bring to boil, stirring until there are no lumps. Remove from heat; stir in potatoes and parsley. Serve parsley potatoes in mounds with well in the center of each. Top with meat sauce. Serves 4-5.

Sweet & Sour Beef

4 c. water
½ c. dried carrots
⅓ c. dried onion
2 T. dried green pepper
1 T. beef bouillon

1 (12-oz.) can beef chunks, undrained and broken up
1 (15-oz.) can tomato sauce
¼ c. brown sugar, packed
2 T. vinegar
1 T. Worcestershire Sauce
2 T. cornstarch
¼ c. water

Combine all ingredients in first column and simmer 20 minutes. Add rest of ingredients, except cornstarch and ¼ cup water, and simmer 5 minutes. Mix cornstarch in ¼ cup water until there are no lumps; stir into beef mixture. Bring back to boil stirring constantly. Simmer 1 minute. Serve over cooked rice. Serves 5-6.

Variation: Add 1 (20-oz.) can pineapple chunks, drained, reserving juice. Add enough water to reserved juice to make required 4 cups liquid. Also add one more tablespoon of cornstarch.

—Adapted recipe from Annette Harkness

Beef Goulash

2 (15-oz.) cans diced tomatoes, undrained
2 (12-oz.) cans beef chunks
1 T. dried onion
1¼ t. sugar
½ t. dried minced garlic
½ t. paprika

¼ t. Worcestershire sauce
¼ t. vinegar
1 bay leaf
optional:
   ¼ c. water
   2 T. cornstarch

Combine all ingredients except water and cornstarch in a saucepan. Simmer 15 minutes to blend flavors. Remove bay leaf. If desired, mix cornstarch into water until there are no lumps. Stir into meat mixture; bring to boil for 2-3 minutes. Serve over hot rice. Serves 4-5.

Curry Beef on Rice

1 (12-oz.) can beef chunks
1 (15-oz.) can diced tomatoes, undrained
2 c. water
½ c. dried apples, chopped in ¼-inch pieces
¼ c. dried onion

2 T. dried celery
2 t. beef bouillon
1-1½ t. curry powder
½ t. dried minced garlic
½ t. sugar
¼ t. turmeric

Pour beef into saucepan and break up. Add rest of ingredients; bring to boil and simmer, uncovered, 20-25 minutes. Serve over hot rice. Serves 4-5.

91

Corned Beef with Parsley Sauce
Because corned beef is salty, this recipe is served on unsalted rice.

1 (12-oz.) can corned beef
1 recipe medium Super Quick White Sauce, pg. 53

1 T. dried parsley
rice, cooked with no salt

Slice corned beef into 10 slices while cold. Gently transfer slices to a saucepan. Add a little water and heat through. Make white sauce and add parsley. Simmer 1 minute. Gently transfer two corned beef slices onto a bed of hot rice. Top with parsley sauce. Serves 4-5.

Corned Beef Hash

4½ c. water
3¼ c. dried potato dices
½ c. dried onion
¾ t. salt
½ t. garlic powder

¼ t. pepper
1 (12-oz.) can corned beef
¼ c. oil
1½ T. dried parsley

Combine ingredients in first column and cook, covered, until liquid is evaporated (at least 10 minutes). Cut corned beef into ¼-inch dices. Brown potato mixture and pepper in hot oil in a large non-stick frying pan. Stir in corned beef; fry 2 minutes more, stirring occasionally to break up corned beef. Stir in parsley and serve. Serves 6.

Creamy Chicken and Green Beans

1 (10-oz.) can cream of chicken soup
½ c. reconstituted dry milk
½ t. thyme

1 (15-oz.) can green beans, drained
1 (10-oz.) can chicken or turkey chunks

In sauce pan blend soup, milk and thyme. Stir in beans. Gently stir in chicken and heat through. Serve over mashed potatoes or hot noodles. Serves 4-5.

Pineapple Chicken

1 c. water (include liquid from canned chicken)
1 c. ketchup
⅓ c. sugar
¼ t. onion powder
¼ t. garlic powder
1 T. soy sauce

½ t. bottled lemon juice
¼ c. water
3 T. cornstarch
1 (20-oz.) can pineapple chunks, drained, reserving ¾ c. juice
1 (10-oz.) can chicken chunks

In medium saucepan combine ingredients in first column, lemon juice and reserved pineapple juice. Bring to boil; remove from heat. Stir cornstarch into ¼ c. water until there are no lumps. Stir into hot pineapple sauce. Return to heat; bring to boil, stirring constantly. Stir in pineapple and chicken; simmer 5 minutes, stirring occasionally. Serve over hot cooked rice. Serves 5-6.
Variation: Add any dry vegetables with needed hydrating water or cut up fresh vegetables to the sauce at the beginning. Simmer sauce and vegetables 10-15 minutes until vegetables are cooked before thickening.

Mushroom Chicken and Noodles

1 (4-oz.) can sliced mushrooms
1 T. dried onion
2 T. flour
1 (12-oz.) can evaporated milk

1 (10-oz.) can cream of mushroom soup
1 (10-oz.) can chicken chunks, broken up
1 T. dried parsley
cooked noodles

Drain juice from mushrooms into a saucepan. Add dried onion and simmer, covered, 10 minutes. In a cup stir flour into a little evaporated milk until there are no lumps. Pour remaining milk, mushroom soup and flour mixture into cooking onion; stir until boiling. Reduce heat; simmer 2 minutes. Add chicken chunks, mushrooms, and parsley, stirring just until combined. Heat through; serve over hot noodles. Serves 6.

Seven Layer Chicken Casserole

1¼ c. water, include juice from meat and corn
2 (8-oz.) cans tomato sauce
½ t. garlic powder
¼ t. salt
1 c. uncooked long grain rice

1 (15-oz.) can corn, undrained
½ (4-oz.) can diced green chiles
1 T. dried onion
1 (10-oz.) can chicken or turkey chunks, broken up
½ (2-oz.) jar bacon pieces

Combine first four ingredients in saucepan; heat until boiling while assembling the rest of the casserole. Spread rice in bottom of greased 2-quart casserole dish; top with canned corn, then chiles. Layer with dried onion, chicken; pour tomato sauce mixture over top. Sprinkle with bacon. Bake, uncovered, at 375° F for 40 minutes. Serves 5-6.   —Adapted recipe from Tatiana Allen

Chicken Broccoli Twist

5 c. water
2 t. chicken bouillon
½ t. garlic powder
3 c. uncooked rotini pasta
¾ c. dried broccoli

½ c. dried diced carrots
1 (10¾-oz.) can cream of chicken soup
1 (10-oz.) can chicken chunks, broken up
⅛ t. pepper
Parmesan cheese

In a saucepan, bring water, bouillon and garlic powder to boil; add pasta, broccoli and carrots. Simmer, covered, 10 minutes. Stir in soup, chicken and pepper. Heat and serve topped with Parmesan. Serves 5-6.

Chicken a la King

3 c. water (include liquid from
    mushrooms and chicken)
2 T. dried green pepper
½ c. Super Quick White Sauce Mix, pg. 53
3 T. flour

1½ t. chicken bouillon
½ t. onion powder
1 (10-12.5-oz.) can chicken chunks, broken up
1 (4-oz) can sliced mushrooms, undrained
1 (2-oz.) bottle pimento, drained (optional)
Biscuits, pg. 59

Soak green pepper in water in saucepan for 15 minutes while preparing biscuits. Whisk in white sauce mix; then flour, bouillon and onion powder. Bring to boil; simmer 1 minute. Add rest of ingredients and bring to boil; serve over biscuits. Serves 4-5.

Hawaiian Haystacks

1 (10-oz.) can chicken or turkey chunks
1 (4-oz.) can sliced mushrooms
1 c. Super Quick White Sauce Mix, pg. 53
1 T. dried parsley
1-1½ t. chicken bouillon
½ t. onion powder
⅛ t. curry powder (optional)

hot cooked rice
Toppings:
    1 (9.5-oz.) can chow mein noodles
    Pineapple chunks, drained
    Hydrated green peas
    Diced tomatoes (summer)
    Shredded coconut
    Slivered almonds

Drain liquid from meat and mushrooms and add enough water to make 2 cups. Heat in saucepan. Whisk in rest of ingredients in first column; bring to boil, while stirring. Simmer 1 min. Add chicken and mushrooms; heat to boiling. Serve over rice with desired toppings. Serves 5-6.

Green Beans and Turkey

1 (10.-oz.) can cream mushroom soup
¼ (5-oz.) bottle processed sharp cheese spread
2 (15-oz.) cans green beans, drained

1 (12-oz.) can turkey chunks, broken up
1 (4-oz.) can sliced mushrooms, drained

Heat mushroom soup and cheese in saucepan until boiling, stirring constantly. Stir in turkey, beans and mushrooms. Serve over instant mashed potatoes or rice. Serves 4-5.

Turkey Cranberry Pancakes

1½ c. Super Quick Mix, pg. 53
1 T. dried whole egg, sifted
½ t. onion powder
1 (12-oz.) can evaporated milk

1 (10-oz.) can turkey chunks, drained, broken up
½ c. cranberry sauce
butter-flavored cooking oil spray
extra cranberry sauce

In mixing bowl whisk together Super Quick Mix, egg and onion powder. Stir in milk until combined. Add turkey and cranberry sauce; stir together. Heat skillet; spray with oil. Cook pancakes, on medium heat, a ¼ cup at a time. Cook 2-3 minutes on each side. Serve warm with extra cranberry sauce on top. Makes 12-14 pancakes.

94

Tuna on Rice

2-2½ c. cooked rice
1-2 (6-oz.) cans tuna

Soy sauce

Serve hot rice on plates. Top with drained tuna. Sprinkle with soy sauce. Serves 4-5.

Creamy Broccoli and Tuna

3 c. uncooked rotini pasta
4 c. water
1 c. dried broccoli
1½ c. water
½ c. Super Quick White Sauce Mix, pg. 53

¼ c. Parmesan cheese
¼ t. garlic powder
½ t. salt
1 (6-oz.) can tuna, drained

Cook pasta and broccoli in 4 cups water for 10 minutes; drain. In another sauce pan, combine 1½ cups water, white sauce mix and rest of ingredients in second column, except tuna. Bring to a boil; simmer 1 minute. Stir in broccoli, pasta and tuna; heat and serve. Serves 4-5.

Complete-meal Tuna Helper

1 pkg. Tuna Helper, prepared
   according to directions
1½ c. extra water

½ c. dried diced carrots
½ c. freeze-dried peas

Prepare Tuna Helper adding extra water and dried vegetables (the margarine is not needed). Simmer, uncovered, 15 minutes instead of 10. Serves 4-5.

Tuna Potato Patties

4 c. dehydrated mashed potatoes, made very stiff
1 (6-oz.) can tuna in water, undrained
1½ T. dried parsley
1 T. dried onion

3 T. mayonnaise
⅛ t. garlic powder
bottled lemon juice
ground pepper
oil

Mix ingredients except lemon juice and pepper and make into 9 patties (about ½ c. each). Fry in oil in non-stick frying pan until lightly brown on both sides. Serve with lemon juice and ground pepper on top.

Tuna Mornay

1 (15-oz.) can corn, well drained
1 c. hydrated freeze-dried peas OR,
    1 (15-oz.) can peas or asparagus,
    well drained
1 (6-oz.) can tuna, drained

1¾ c. water
1 heaped c. Super Quick White Sauce Mix, pg. 53
1 bay leaf
½ t. onion powder
½ (5-oz.) bottle processed sharp cheese spread

Sprinkle corn evenly in bottom of greased 8x12-inch pan. Top with peas or asparagus, then tuna. Combine water, white sauce mix, bay leaf and onion powder in saucepan; bring to boil on medium heat, stirring constantly. Lower heat and boil 1 minute. Remove bay leaf and pour white sauce over top of casserole. Dot with cheese. Bake at 375° F for 30 minutes. Serves 5.
Option: In place of processed cheese spread, hydrate 1 c. of freeze-dried cheese in ½ c. lukewarm water while preparing the recipe. Sprinkle hydrated cheese over top of dish before baking.

—Adapted recipe from Anna Probert

Tuna Rice Bake

1½ c. water
1 (12-oz.) can evaporated milk
1 (8-oz.) bottle processed sharp cheese spread
1½ c. long grain rice

1 T. dried parsley
1 T. dried onion
½ t. dry mustard
1 (6-oz.) can tuna, drained

In a small saucepan, combine water and evaporated milk; bring to a boil on medium heat. Add cheese; stir until melted. Mix in rest of ingredients. Pour into greased 2½-quart baking dish. Cover and bake at 350° F for 45 minutes or until rice is tender. Serves 6.

Salmon Patties

1 T. dried whole egg, sifted
2 T. water
1 (15-oz.) can salmon

½ c. cornmeal
1 T. flour
oil

Whisk together egg and water until there are no lumps. Drain salmon, reserving liquid. Remove bones. Combine cornmeal and flour; add to egg mixture with salmon. Stir in enough reserved liquid from salmon to moisten ingredients well. Form into patties. Fry in oil. Makes 6, 3-inch patties.

— Adapted recipe from Shannon Slinker

Salmon Loaf

1 (15-oz.) can pink salmon, undrained
1 c. saltine cracker crumbs
½ c. evaporated milk

1 T. dried onion
1 T. dried parsley
1 t. dried tarragon
2 T. bottled lemon juice

Put salmon in a bowl and remove bones. Add rest of ingredients; stir until combined. Spread in greased 8x4-inch bread pan; bake, uncovered, at 375° F for 40 minutes. Serve with fried potato dices. Serves 4-5.

Side Dishes

Fried Potatoes

3 c. water
2 c. dried potato dices or hash browns

¼ c. oil
salt and pepper

Simmer potatoes in water for 10 minutes until all the water is absorbed. Heat oil in non-stick frying pan; fry potatoes until golden brown. Salt and pepper to taste as they cook. Serves 4.

Polenta

3½ c. water
1 c. cornmeal

1½ t. chicken bouillon

Combine cornmeal with ½ cup water. Bring 3 cups water to boil with bouillon. Add cornmeal; stir until lumps dissolve and mixture comes to boil. Reduce heat to medium-low; cover and simmer 15 minutes. Serve mounded like mashed potatoes. Serves 5-6.
Variations: Add ¼ t. onion powder and ⅓-½ cup Parmesan cheese.

Hush Puppies

1¼ c. cornmeal
¼ c. flour
1 T. dried whole egg, sifted
¾ t. salt
½ t. baking soda
¼ t. black pepper

⅛ t. cayenne pepper
2 T. hydrated dried onion
¾ c. evaporated milk
2 T. water
1 T. bottled lemon juice
oil

Mix together all dry ingredients; stir in hydrated onion. Add milk, water and lemon juice to dry mixture; stir until well combined. Allow to stand 2-3 minutes. Drop by tablespoons into hot oil. Fry until golden brown on all sides. Drain on paper towels and serve immediately. Makes about 2 dozen.

Corn Fritters

1½ c. whole wheat flour
1 T. baking powder
1 T. dried whole egg, sifted
¾ t. salt

1 (15-oz.) can corn, reserving liquid
reconstituted dry milk
2 T. water
oil

Add milk to corn liquid to measure 1 cup. Whisk together dry ingredients in a bowl. Add corn, water and milk mixture; stir until combined. Drop batter by heaping tablespoons into deep hot oil, 350° F. Fry until golden brown, 3-3½ minutes. Drain on paper towels. Makes 1½-2 dozen. Great with hot pepper sauce!
Creamed corn variation: Substitute can of creamed corn for corn; add ¼ cup milk for liquid.

Spanish Rice

1 T. oil
1 c. uncooked long grain rice
1½ c. water
1 (8-oz.) can tomato sauce

½ (4-oz.) can diced green chiles
2 t. chicken bouillon
¼ t. dried minced garlic
¼ t. cumin

In saucepan, lightly brown rice in oil on medium-high heat. Add rest of ingredients and simmer, covered, 20 minutes until liquid is absorbed. Serves 4-5.

Garden Variation: Substitute 2 medium tomatoes, diced and ¼ cup diced green peppers for tomato sauce and diced green chiles.

Tomato Risotto

1 T. oil
1 c. uncooked long grain rice
1½ c. water
1 (15-oz.) can diced tomatoes, undrained
¼ c. dried onion

1½ t. chicken bouillon
⅛ t. dried basil
1 bay leaf
Parmesan cheese

In saucepan lightly brown rice in oil on medium-high heat. Add rest of ingredients except cheese and simmer, covered, 20 minutes or until liquid is absorbed. Remove bay leaf; serve hot, sprinkled with Parmesan cheese. Serves 5-6.

For a complete meal: Add ½ (2-oz.) jar bacon pieces or canned chicken chunks, drained, and other vegetables.

Garden Variation: Substitute 4 diced, medium tomatoes for canned tomatoes. May also add sliced or diced zucchini.

Tomatoes on-the-side

Drain liquid from 1 (15-oz.) can diced tomatoes into a saucepan. Add 1 teaspoon dried onion and 1 teaspoon powdered butter or olive oil and cook until most of the liquid is gone. Add tomatoes and heat through. Season with salt and pepper to taste and serve as a side dish to scrambled eggs or any main dish meal. Serves 4.

Desserts

Creamed Rice

4 c. reconstituted dry milk
⅓ c. sugar
¾ c. uncooked long grain rice

1 T. cornstarch
¼ c. raisins
1 t. vanilla

Bring milk and sugar to boil on medium heat. Stir cornstarch into rice; add to boiling mixture. Stir in raisins; simmer, uncovered, on medium-low heat, stirring frequently, about 20-25 minutes. Remove from heat; add vanilla. Cover with clear food wrap touching surface to prevent skin from forming on top; cool. This will thicken as it cools. Stir in additional milk if too thick. Serve warm or cold. Serves 4-6.

Chocolate Pudding Cake

1½ c. Super Quick Mix, pg. 53
½ c. sugar
2 T. cocoa
⅔ c. reconstituted dry milk

1 t. vanilla
¾ c. brown sugar, packed
2 T. cocoa
1½ c. boiling water

Stir together first 3 ingredients in ungreased 8-inch square pan until well combined. Add milk and vanilla; stir well. Combine brown sugar and cocoa; add boiling water and gently pour over cake mixture. Do not stir. Bake at 350° F for 35-40 minutes until edges pull away from pan. Cool in pan 15 minutes. Serve warm.

Nutty Caramel Pudding Cake

1¼ c. Super Quick Mix, pg. 53
⅓ c. brown sugar, packed
½ c. chopped nuts
½ c. raisins OR hydrated and chopped
    dried apples
¾ c. reconstituted dry milk

Brown Sugar Topping
½ c. brown sugar, packed
1 T. powdered butter
2 c. boiling water

Spray 8x12-inch glass baking dish with cooking spray oil. Combine first 4 ingredients. Add milk, blend well and pour into pan. Combine ingredients for Brown Sugar Topping with whisk. Pour gently over top of cake. Bake at 350° F for 30 minutes until cake springs back when lightly touched. Cool in pan 15 minutes before serving.

Pineapple Pudding Cake: Substitute 1 cup drained crushed pineapple (reserve liquid) in place of nuts and dried fruit. May substitute white sugar in place of brown if desired. Include reserved pineapple juice in 2 cups boiling liquid poured over the top.

Light and Easy Fruit Cobbler

½ c. sugar
1 T. cornstarch
1 (29-oz.) can fruit, including juice
1 c. flour (½ white, ½ whole wheat)
2 T. sugar

1½ t. baking powder
½ t. salt
¼ c. shortening
½ c. reconstituted dry milk
cinnamon and nutmeg

Combine sugar and cornstarch in saucepan. Add juice from canned fruit and bring to boil. Add fruit and heat to boiling; remove from heat. Mix dry ingredients together. Blend in shortening until mixture resembles cornmeal. Stir in milk to make soft dough. Pour fruit mixture into 8x8-inch baking dish. Sprinkle with cinnamon and nutmeg. Drop dough by tablespoons on top. Bake at 400° F for 20-25 minutes.

Garden Variation: Combine ⅔-1 cup sugar and 1 tablespoon cornstarch. Add 1 cup water and bring to boil. Add 2 cups prepared fresh fruit and bring to boil. Remove from heat. Continue as above.

Canned Pie Filling Variation: Substitute 1 (28-oz.) can pie filling for cooked fruit; add a little water to thin slightly.

—Adapted recipe from Nancy Scott

Bread Pudding

2½ c. reconstituted dry milk
½ c. raisins
½ c. hydrated and drained dried apples,
    chopped (optional)
½ c. sugar
¼ c. dried whole egg, sifted
2 T. butter powder, sifted

1 t. cinnamon
¼ t. nutmeg
⅛ t. salt
2 t. vanilla
4 c. stale whole wheat bread cubes
    (about 5 slices cut in ½-inch cubes)

In a saucepan heat milk, raisins and apples until hot; remove from heat. In a bowl, whisk together dry ingredients; whisk into hot milk. Stir in vanilla. Place bread cubes in a large bowl; pour milk mixture over cubes. Stir and let stand 10 minutes to allow bread to soak. Pour into 2 greased 8x4-inch bread pans. Bake at 350° F for 25-30 minutes until knife inserted in middle comes out clean. Serve warm. Serves 4-6.

Optional Lemon Sauce:

¾ c. sugar
½ c. bottled lemon juice

2 T. cornstarch
1½ t. water

In saucepan combine sugar and lemon juice; bring to boil, stirring constantly. Stir together cornstarch and water in a cup, until there are no lumps. Whisk cornstarch mixture into lemon sauce. Heat; stirring constantly, until thickened. Simmer 1 minute.

Apricot Delight

1 (15-oz.) can apricot halves, drained
1½ c. reconstituted dry milk
ground nutmeg, if desired

½ c. rounded, vanilla instant pudding OR
   1 (3⅓-oz.) pkg. vanilla instant pudding
⅛ t. almond flavoring (optional)

Dice and mash apricots. Add milk and pudding and whip until smooth and thickened. Sprinkle with nutmeg.

Variation: Use other canned fruit in place of apricots.

—Tatiana Allen

Lemon Icebox Dessert

1 (12-oz.) can evaporated milk, well chilled
¾ c. sugar
¼ c. bottled lemon juice

¾ c. graham cracker crumbs
2 T. sugar

Combine graham cracker crumbs and 2 tablespoons sugar. Reserve 2 tablespoons for topping. Sprinkle rest of mixture into bottom of 9-inch square baking pan.

Whip evaporated milk until stiff. Add ¾ c. sugar and lemon juice. Continue whipping until well mixed. Pour into pan on top of crumbs and sprinkle with reserved crumbs. Freeze (during freezing weather) 3-4 hours to blend flavors. Serves 6-8.

Creamy Jell-O™ Dessert or Pie

1 (3-oz. pkg.) flavored gelatin, any flavor
½ c. boiling water
1 c. evaporated milk

1 T. bottled lemon juice
2 T. sugar
graham cracker or flaky pie crust, optional

In small bowl, dissolve flavored gelatin in boiling water. While it cools to room temperature, beat evaporated milk until frothy; add lemon juice and sugar and beat until triple in size. Beat in cooled gelatin. Pour immediately into dessert cups or pie crust. Chill 30 minutes to 1 hour for dessert; 2-3 hours for pie.

Impossible Pumpkin Pie

1 c. Super Quick Mix, pg. 53
½ c. sugar
2 T. dried whole egg, sifted
1 t. cinnamon
½ t. ginger

¼ t. cloves
1 (15-oz.) can pumpkin or 1/2 (29-oz.) can
1 (12-oz.) can evaporated milk
¼ c. water
2 t. vanilla

Grease a 10-inch pie pan. Whisk dry ingredients together. Add rest of ingredients and whisk until combined. Pour into pie plate and bake at 350° F for 50-55 minutes or until knife inserted in center comes out clean. Serve with Evaporated Milk Whipped Topping below.

Evaporated Milk Whipped Topping (unusually good whipped cream substitute)

1 c. evaporated milk
¼-½ c. powdered sugar

1 t. vanilla

Pour evaporated milk into small mixing bowl. Chill for about 30 minutes. Beat for 1 minute or until very frothy. Gradually add sugar and vanilla; continue beating for 2 minutes or until mixture is stiff. Serve immediately. Makes 3 cups.

For Whipped Evaporated Milk that holds up to 30 minutes: Sprinkle 1 teaspoon gelatin over 2 tablespoons very hot water in small bowl; stir until dissolved. Add to evaporated milk before chilling. After whipping, cover and chill for up to 30 minutes.

Idaho Bicentennial Pie

2 c. cooked pinto or red beans, mashed
1 (12-oz.) can evaporated milk
2 T. water
1 c. sugar
2 T. dried whole egg, sifted

1 t. cinnamon
½ t. nutmeg
½ t. salt
¼ t. ground cloves
1 (9-inch) unbaked pie shell

Combine beans and milk; blend until smooth. Beat in rest of ingredients; pour into pie shell. Bake at 375° F for 1 hour or until knife inserted in center comes out clean. Serve with Evaporated Milk Whipped Topping, pg. 102.

Coconut Pinto Pie

1 c. mashed cooked pinto beans
1 c. evaporated milk
2 T. water
1 c. sugar

2 T. dried whole egg, sifted
½ c. flaked coconut
⅛ t. salt
1 (8-inch) unbaked pie shell

Combine beans and milk; blend until smooth. Beat in rest of ingredients and pour into pie shell. Bake at 350° F for 45 minutes. Serve with Evaporated Milk Whipped Topping, pg. 102.

Pat-in-the-Pan Pie Crust (no need to roll out)

1¼ c. flour
1½ t. sugar
1 t. salt

⅓ c. oil
¼ c. reconstituted dry milk

Mix dry ingredients together in pie pan. In a bowl, whip together oil and milk with fork. Pour oil mixture over dry ingredients and mix together. Finish mixing with hands. Pat dough into the bottom and up the sides of a 9-inch pie pan. Flute the edges. Prick the bottom with a fork. Bake 10 minutes at 450° F. If baking with filling, do not prick. Best when eaten the same day as filled.

—Tresa Hansen

Fabulous Oil Pie Crust

2⅓ c. flour
2¼ t. sugar
1½ t. salt

⅔ c. oil
½ c. reconstituted dry milk

Mix dry ingredients together. Pour in oil and milk and mix with fork until well combined. Dough will appear dry at first. Keep stirring, then knead to form a ball. Roll between two pieces of wax paper. To keep paper from slipping as you roll dough out, put a drop of water on counter. Makes a double 10-inch crust. For single crusts, bake at 450° F for 10 minutes.

Cooked Pudding/Pie Filling Mix

This delicious mix is the least expensive way to enjoy cooked pudding. Pudding recipes are made even richer by substituting ½ cup evaporated milk for the ½ cup water in the recipe.

5⅓ c. instant dry milk
4 c. sugar
1½ c. cornstarch
1 c. dried whole egg, sifted

1 c. powdered butter, sifted
1 c. flour
4 t. salt

Mix above ingredients together with a whisk. Store large mix in #10 can.

Vanilla Pudding: Whisk 1 c. of mix into 2¼ c. very warm water in a saucepan. Stir on medium-high heat until boiling. Boil 1 min. Remove from heat; add 1½ t. vanilla. Cool with plastic wrap touching surface of pudding to prevent skin from forming. Serve plain or with fruit. Makes 3 cups.

Pie Filling: Reduce water by ¼ c.

Chocolate Pudding: To recipe for vanilla pudding, add additional 2 T. sugar and 2 T. cocoa.

Coconut Pudding: To recipe for vanilla pudding, add vanilla or coconut flavoring. Add ½ c. shredded coconut to cooled pudding; chill further to blend flavors.

Eggnog Pudding: Substitute ½ t. rum flavoring for vanilla in vanilla pudding; add ¼ t. nutmeg.

Maple Nut Pudding : Substitute maple flavoring for vanilla in vanilla pudding. May use brown sugar in place of white sugar. Add ¼-½ c. chopped walnuts to cooled pudding and chill further.

Butterscotch Pudding: Whisk together 1½ T. brown sugar and 1 t. butter powder. Add to 1 c. pudding mix; follow directions for vanilla recipe. Substitute ½ t. butterscotch flavoring for vanilla.

Apple Crisp

6 c. dried apple slices
4½ c. boiling water
1 c. quick oats
¼ c. flour

½ c. brown sugar, packed, divided
1 t. cinnamon
½ c. chopped nuts or coconut
½ c. butter flavored shortening

Pour water over apples; let stand 5 minutes. Pour apples and water in 8x12-inch glass baking dish; sprinkle with ¼ c. brown sugar. Combine rest of ingredients including remaining ¼ c. brown sugar; sprinkle over apples. Bake at 350° F for 45 minutes.

Cakes

High altitude adjustments:
*   For 3,000 ft. reduce sugar by 1 T. for each cup, leavening by ⅛ t. for each teaspoon and add 1 T. liquid or each cup.*
*   For 5,000 ft. double above amounts.*

Gingerbread

1¼ c. reconstituted dry milk
1¼ T. bottled lemon juice
3 c. whole wheat flour
2 T. dried whole egg, sifted
1 t. ginger
1 t. cinnamon

¾ t. soda
½ t. salt
½ t. ground cloves
¾ c. sugar
⅔ c. oil
1 c. molasses

Sour milk by putting 1¼ T. lemon juice in bottom of measuring cup. Fill to 1¼ cup with reconstituted dry milk. Let stand at room temperature until called for in recipe.

Combine dry ingredients, except sugar, together in a bowl. In another bowl, stir together sugar, milk, oil and molasses for 1 minute. Stir in dry ingredients until combined and beat 1 minute. Pour into greased 9x13-inch cake pan. Bake at 350° F for 35 minutes. Serve topped with applesauce and Evaporated Milk Whipped Topping, pg. 102.

Oatmeal Cake

1½ c. whole wheat flour, finely ground
1 c. quick cooking oats
1 c. brown sugar, packed
½ c. sugar
2 T dried whole egg, sifted
1½ t. baking soda

1 t. cinnamon
½ t. salt
½ t. nutmeg
½ c. shortening
1¼ c. water
2 T. molasses

Combine all ingredients in a large mixing bowl; beat on medium speed for 3 minutes (450 strokes by hand with a whisk). Pour into a greased and floured 9x13-inch pan. Bake at 350° F for 35-40 minutes until cake is done (toothpick inserted in center comes out clean.) Cool.
Variation #1: Add 1 cup raisins or chopped nuts.
Variation #2: Cool cake slightly and frost with the following topping and return to oven for 7 minutes until topping bubbles:

½ c. butter flavored shortening
1 c. brown sugar, packed
⅓ c. evaporated milk

1 c. coconut
1 c. nuts, chopped
1 t. vanilla

Melt shortening and blend in sugar. Stir in remaining ingredients. Bring to boil, stirring.

Chocolate Cake

2¼ t. vinegar +reconstituted dry milk
    to make ¾ c. (Let stand 5 minutes)
2 c. whole wheat flour, finely ground
2 c. sugar
¾ c. cocoa
2 T. dried whole egg, sifted

1 t. salt
1 t. baking soda
½ t. baking powder
¾ c. shortening
1 c. water
1 t. vanilla

Combine all ingredients in a large bowl; beat with mixer at medium speed for 3 minutes (450 strokes by hand with whisk). Pour into greased 9x13-inch pan. Bake at 350° F for 40-45 minutes until cake is done (toothpick inserted in center comes out clean). Cool. Sprinkle with powdered sugar, frost or serve topped with canned cherry pie filling and imitation whipped cream.

Chocolate Fudge Frosting

½ c. butter flavored shortening
⅔ c. cocoa
3 c. powdered sugar

⅓ c. reconstituted dry milk
1 t. vanilla

Melt shortening; stir in cocoa. Add powdered sugar, milk and vanilla, beating until spreadable. Add additional milk if needed. Makes 2 cups.

Applesauce Cake

2 ½ c. whole wheat flour, finely ground
2 c. sugar
2 T. dried whole egg, sifted
1½ t. salt
1½ t. baking soda
¼ t. baking powder
¼ t. cinnamon

¼ t. nutmeg
1½ c. applesauce
½ c. shortening
¾ c. water
1 c. raisins
½ c. chopped walnuts

Combine all ingredients in a large bowl; beat with mixer at medium speed for 3 minutes (450 strokes by hand with whisk). Pour into greased 9x13-inch pan. Bake at 350° F for 60-65 minutes until cake is done (toothpick inserted in center comes out clean). Cool. Frost or serve topped with applesauce and imitation whipped cream.

Old Fruit Cake

1 qt. of old bottled fruit, pureed OR
    4 c. canned fruit and juice, pureed
1 c. oil
2 c. sugar
4 c. flour (whole wheat or white)

4 t. baking soda
2 t. cinnamon
1 t. salt
1 t. nutmeg
1 t. ground cloves

In bowl, beat oil into fruit puree. Mix together dry ingredients; add to fruit mixture and beat until combined. Bake in greased and floured 9x13-inch pan at 350° F for 45-55 minutes. Cool and top with Penuche Frosting below.

Optional: Add crushed nuts, raisins or coconut to this cake and omit frosting.

Penuche Frosting:

¼ c. reconstituted dry milk OR evaporated milk
½ c. brown sugar, packed
½ c. butter flavored shortening

2½-3 c. powdered sugar
1 t. vanilla

Dissolve brown sugar in milk in saucepan. Add shortening and boil 1 minute. Remove from heat; add rest of ingredients, beating until powdered sugar lumps are gone and frosting is spreading consistency.

—Marianna Robbins

Apple Slice Cake

2 c. dried apples
2 c. water
1½ c. white flour
1½ c. whole wheat flour
2 c. sugar
2 T. dried whole egg, sifted

1 t. baking soda
1 t. salt
1 t. cinnamon
1 t. allspice
⅔ c. oil
2 t. vanilla

Hydrate apples in water while measuring rest of ingredients and preparing topping below. In a bowl, whisk together dry ingredients. Drain apples reserving 1 cup of liquid. Stir apples into dry ingredients. Add oil and vanilla to water; pour into apple mixture and lightly stir just until combined. Spread out in greased 9x13-inch pan. Sprinkle with topping below. Bake at 350° F for 30-35 minutes.

Topping:

1 c. brown sugar, packed
1 c. nuts

½ c. butter flavored shortening

Cut shortening into sugar. Add nuts and combine.

—Adapted recipe from Tresa Hansen

Maple Nut Cake

½ c. shortening
2 c. sugar
1 c. mashed pinto beans
2 T. dried whole egg
1 t. maple extract
3 c. flour (whole wheat or white)

¼ t. baking powder
½ c. reconstituted dry milk
¼ c. water
½ c. coconut
½ c. nuts

Cream together the first 5 ingredients. Beat for 2 minutes. Combine flour and baking powder. Combine milk and water. Add dry ingredients alternately with milk mixture. Mix until smooth. Fold in coconut and nuts. Bake in greased 9x13-inch cake pan at 350° F for 45 minutes.
Frosting: Mix ¾ c. bean puree, 2 T. buttered flavored shortening, and powdered sugar until the desired consistency is reached. Add any desired flavorings.

Apple Surprise Cake

½ c. shortening
1 c. sugar
¼ c. water
2 T. dried whole egg
1 c. pinto bean puree
1 c. apple sauce
1½ t. vanilla
2 c. flour (whole wheat or white)

2 t. baking powder
1 t. cinnamon
½ t. nutmeg
¼ t. salt
¼ t. ground cloves
2 c. hydrated and drained dried apples, chopped
¾ c. raisins
¼ c. chopped nuts

Cream shortening and sugar until light and fluffy. Add water and egg; beat until light. Stir in bean puree, apple sauce and vanilla. Combine dry ingredients; add to bean mixture. Stir in chopped apples, raisins and nuts. Pour into greased 9x13-inch pan. Bake at 375° F for 45-50 minutes.

Amazing Pinto Bean Cupcakes

1 c. warm pinto beans,
    cooked, drained, and mashed
2 c. flour (whole wheat or white)
1¼ c. sugar
2½ t. baking powder
2 T. dried whole egg, sifted
1 t. salt
1 t. cinnamon

½ t. ground cloves
½ t. nutmeg
½ c. shortening
¾ c. reconstituted dry milk
1 t. molasses
¼ c. water
¼ c. reconstituted dry milk
1 t. vanilla

Grease cupcake pans or line with liners. Combine all dry ingredients in a mixing bowl. Add shortening, ¾ cup milk and molasses. Beat 2 minutes. Add water, ¼ cup milk, warm beans and vanilla. Beat 2 more minutes. Fill cups and bake at 400° F for 20 minutes. Cool. Frost or serve hot and buttered. Makes 12 cupcakes.

—Charlotte Putman

Cookies & Treats

Cookies baked on light colored baking sheets do not get too dark.

Because whole wheat flour can vary in moisture content, it may be necessary to add a little more liquid or more flour to the cookie recipes below.

Cookies

Chocolate Chip Cookies

1 c. shortening
¾ c. sugar
¾ c. brown sugar, packed
2 T. dried whole egg
¼ c. water
2 T. reconstituted dry milk
1 t. vanilla

3 c. whole wheat flour
½ t. baking soda
½ t. salt
2 c. chocolate chips
½ c. walnuts, chopped (optional)

Put ingredients in first column in bowl; mix together just until combined. (Shortening will be in small lumps.) Mix dry ingredients together and blend into shortening mixture just until combined. Add chocolate chips and nuts. Drop by tablespoons onto an ungreased cookie sheet. Bake at 375° F for 10-12 minutes. Makes 3 dozen.

***Chocolate Chip Bars*:** Add ½ teaspoon baking powder and increase milk to ¼ cup. Press into ungreased 9x13-inch shiny cake pan. Bake at 350° F for 25 minutes.

Soft Peanut Butter Cookies

1 c. shortening
2½ c. brown sugar, packed
6 T. reconstituted dry milk
2 T. dried whole egg
¼ c. water

1½ c. peanut butter
1 T. vanilla
3½ c. whole wheat flour
1½ t. baking soda
1 t. salt

Put ingredients in first column, peanut butter and vanilla in bowl; mix together just until combined. (Shortening will be in small lumps.) Mix dry ingredients together and blend into shortening mixture just until combined. Drop by tablespoons onto ungreased cookie sheet. Make light crisscross on top of each cookie with fork. Bake at 375° F for 7-8 minutes; just until set. Allow to cool 2 minutes on cookie sheet before removing to cooling rack. Makes 3 dozen.

Chewy Oatmeal Cookies

1 c. shortening
1 c. white sugar
1 c. brown sugar, packed
2 T. dried whole egg
¼ c. water
2 t. vanilla

2 c. whole wheat flour
¾ t. baking soda
½ t. salt
1½ c. quick cooking oatmeal

Put ingredients in first column in bowl; mix together just until combined. (Shortening will be in small lumps.) Mix flour, baking powder, soda and salt together and blend into shortening mixture. Blend in oatmeal; dough should be crumbly but stick together when formed into balls. Form into 1¼-inch balls: bake on ungreased cookie sheet at 375° F for 10-12 minutes. Allow to cool 2 minutes before removing from tray. Makes 3 dozen.

Oatmeal Chocolate Chip Cookies

¾ c. shortening
1½ c. brown sugar, packed
2 T. dried whole egg
¼ c. water
1 t. vanilla

1¼ c. whole wheat flour
½ t. baking soda
½ t. salt
2 c. oatmeal
1 c. chocolate chips
raisins or dried apricots, chopped (optional)

Put ingredients in first column in bowl; mix together just until combined. (Shortening will be in small lumps.) Mix together flour, soda and salt; blend into shortening mixture. Stir in oats, chocolate chips and fruit, if desired. Drop onto lightly greased cookie sheet. Bake at 350° F for 12 minutes. Makes 4 dozen.

Gingersnaps

1 c. brown sugar, packed
¾ c. oil
¼ c. molasses
1 T. dried whole egg
2 T. water
2 c. whole wheat flour

2 t. baking soda
1 t. ground cinnamon
1 t. ground ginger
½ t. ground cloves
¼ t. salt

Combine first 5 ingredients. Stir together dry ingredients and gradually blend into molasses mixture. Use about 1 tablespoon of dough to form 1¼-inch balls. Roll in granulated sugar; place on greased cookie sheet about 2 inches apart. Bake at 375° F for 10 minutes. Makes 4 dozen.

Boiled Raisin Cookies

1½ c. raisins
1 c. water
1½ c. sugar
1 c. shortening
3 T. dried whole egg
6 T. water

1 t. vanilla
½ t. salt
3½ c. whole wheat flour
1 t. baking powder
1 t. baking soda

Boil raisins in the 1 cup of water until water is absorbed; cool. Meanwhile, combine rest of ingredients in first column and vanilla just until combined. Mix together dry ingredients and blend into shortening mixture. Make 1-inch balls; roll in sugar. Bake on greased cookie sheet at 350° F for 10-15 minutes. Makes about 5 dozen.

Snickerdoodles

1 c. shortening
1½ c. sugar
2 T. dried whole egg
¼ c. water
2¾ c. whole wheat flour

2 t. cream of tartar
1 t. baking soda
¼ t. salt
2 T. sugar
2 t. cinnamon

Put first 4 ingredients in a bowl; mix together just until combined. Mix together dry ingredients except 2 tablespoons sugar and cinnamon. Blend into shortening mixture. Combine last sugar and cinnamon together in a small bowl. Shape dough into 1-inch balls; roll in cinnamon sugar. Bake on greased cookie sheet at 400° F for 8-10 minutes. Makes about 2½ dozen.

Applesauce Cookies

¾ c. shortening
1½ c. brown sugar, packed
1 T. dried whole egg
2 T. water
3 c. whole wheat flour
1½ t. baking powder

¾ t. salt
¾ t. baking soda
1½ t. cinnamon
¼ t. nutmeg
1½ c. thick, unsweetened applesauce
1½ c. raisins

Put first 4 ingredients in a bowl; mix together just until combined. Mix together dry ingredients; add alternately with applesauce. (If applesauce is thin add a little more flour.) Drop by tablespoons on greased cookie sheet. Bake 350° F for 12-15 minutes. Makes 3 dozen.

Coconut Macaroons

⅔ c. sugar
¼ c. white flour
2 T. + 2 t. dried egg whites

2⅔ c. flaked coconut
¼ c. + 2 t. water
1 t. vanilla

Combine ingredients in first column; stir in coconut. Combine vanilla and water; add to dry ingredients. Combine well. Bake on ungreased cookie sheet at 350° F for 20 minutes. Makes 14.

Rich Coconut Macaroons

5⅓ c. (14-oz.) flaked coconut
2 t. vanilla

1 (14-oz.) can sweetened condensed milk

Combine ingredients and drop by teaspoons onto well- greased cookie sheet. Bake at 350° F 10-12 minutes until golden. Allow to stand 1 minute; remove from cookie sheet to cool. Makes about 4 dozen.

Pumpkin Cookies

2 c. sugar
½ c. oil or shortening
1 T. dried whole egg, sifted
2 T. water
1 (15-oz.) can pumpkin
1 t. vanilla

2½ c. whole wheat flour
1 t. each baking powder AND baking soda
1 t. salt
1½ t. cinnamon
½ t. nutmeg
¼ t. allspice
1 c. raisins, nuts or chocolate chips

Put ingredients in first column in a bowl; mix together. Mix dry ingredients together and add to pumpkin mixture, combining well. Stir in raisins, nuts or chocolate chips. Drop tablespoons onto greased cookie sheet. Bake at 375° for 12-14 minutes. Makes 3 dozen.

For Pumpkin Bread: Pour batter into 1 greased 8 ½x4½-inch loaf pan and bake at 350° F for 1-1¼ hours. Check for doneness with a toothpick.

Tip: This recipe can be doubled using a (29-oz.) can of pumpkin and either baked as cookies, or set aside part of recipe (2⅔ c. batter) in a greased 8½x4½-inch loaf pan, until the cookies are baked, then bake separately.

Pumpkin Squares

1 (15-oz.) can pumpkin
1⅔ c. sugar
¼ c. dried whole egg, sifted
½ c. water
1 c. oil

2 c. whole wheat flour
1 t. salt
2 t. baking powder
2 t. cinnamon

Mix together ingredients in first column. Mix dry ingredients together and blend into first mixture. Pour into ungreased large cookie sheet with 1-inch sides. Bake at 350° F for 25-30 minutes. Frost when cool with icing below. This recipe can also be cooked in a 9x13-inch cake pan for 30-35 minutes and iced with half the icing recipe below.

—Julie Beckstrand

Light and Fluffy Icing:

4 c. powdered sugar
1 c. shortening

3 T. water
1 t. vanilla

Beat together 1 cup powdered sugar with shortening, 2 tablespoons water and vanilla for 1 minute. Add rest of powdered sugar and water and beat for further minute. Spread on pumpkin bars before cutting.

—Laurel Rapp

Peanut Butter Oatmeal Bars

½ c. shortening
⅔ c. peanut butter
1⅓ c. brown sugar, packed
2 T. dried whole egg
¼ c. water

3 T. reconstituted dry milk
1¼ t. vanilla
1¾ c. whole wheat flour
½ t. baking soda
⅔ c. quick cooking oatmeal

Combine ingredients in first column, milk and vanilla just until combined. (Shortening will be in small lumps.) Stir together flour and soda; blend into shortening mixture. Add oatmeal and blend. Spread into lightly greased 9x13-inch pan. Bake at 375° F for 15-18 minutes. Cool. Cut into squares.

Cherry Coconut Bars

⅓ c. sugar
¼ c. shortening
1¼ c. white flour

¼ t. salt
1½ c. flaked coconut
¼ c. water
1 (21-oz.) can cherry pie filling

Cream together sugar and shortening. Combine flour and salt; blend into sugar mixture. Mix in coconut and water. Pat 1¾ c. into bottom of 9-inch square pan. Spread filling on top. Top with rest of crumb mixture. Bake at 350° F for 25-30 minutes. Cool; cut into 16 squares.

Chocolate Brownies

2 c. sugar
½ c. cocoa
1½ c. shortening
¼ c. dried whole egg
¼ c. water

1 T. vanilla
½ t. salt
2 c. whole wheat flour
1¼ c. evaporated milk
1 c. chopped walnuts, optional

Combine all ingredients except flour, milk and nuts. Alternately add flour and milk beating slowly just until blended. Fold in nuts. Spread in greased 9x13-inch baking pan. Bake at 350° F for 25 minutes. Cool and frost with Creamy Chocolate Frosting below. Allow frosting to set for 10 minutes. Cut into 24 bars.

Creamy Chocolate Frosting: Melt ¾ cup semi-sweet chocolate chips with 3 tablespoons shortening in small saucepan on low heat. Stir in ¼ cup evaporated milk leftover from brownie recipe above. Blend in 2 cups sifted powdered sugar and beat until smooth. Spread on brownies while frosting is warm. Allow frosting to set 10 minutes before cutting.

Treats

Peanut Butter Kisses

¼ c. peanut butter
½ c. honey

1 c. (or more) dry milk
½ c. chopped nuts

Mix together honey and peanut butter until smooth. Gradually add milk. Fold in nuts. Form into a long roll and cut into pieces. Makes about 30 pieces.

Fast Drop Doughnuts

2 c. Favorite Roll Mix, pg. 53
¼ c. sugar
2 T. dried whole egg, sifted
1½ t. baking powder
1 t. cinnamon

¼ t. nutmeg
1 c. + 2 T. reconstituted dry milk
1¾ t. vanilla
oil

Whisk together dry ingredients; stir in milk and vanilla just until combined. Drop by heaping teaspoonfuls into hot oil (325° F). Cook for 2-3 minutes; turn once until lightly browned on both sides. Drain on paper towel and roll in cinnamon sugar. Makes about 25-30.

Australian Pikelets

Make Super Quick Pancakes, pg. 50 into 2-inch pancakes. Cool. Spread with jam and top with Evaporated Milk Whipped Topping, pg. 102.

English Scones

Make rolled biscuits, pg. 59; cool. Split cold biscuits in half, spread with jam or jelly and top with dollop of Evaporated Milk Whipped Topping, pg. 102.

Funnel Cakes

3 c. Favorite Roll Mix, pg. 53
1 T. sugar
1 t. baking powder
3 T. dried whole egg, sifted

2½ c. reconstituted dry milk
1 T. vanilla
oil
funnel with ½-inch hole
powdered sugar

Whisk dry ingredients together. Add milk and vanilla; beat 1 minute. Let stand while heating oil (350° F) in 7-inch saucepan. With finger over funnel hole, fill funnel with ⅔ cup batter. Hold funnel over oil and remove finger, slowly moving funnel in a 7-inch circle then back and forth across the center. Keep the stream of batter as steady as possible. Cook until light brown, about 1 minute, on each side. Drain on a paper towel. Sprinkle with powdered sugar. Serve warm. Makes 7-8, 7-inch cakes.

Apple Fritters

1½ whole wheat flour
1 T. baking powder
1 T. dried whole egg, sifted
2 t. sugar
¾ t. salt
1¾ c. hydrated dried apple

1 c. reconstituted dry milk
2 T. water
½ t. vanilla
oil
cinnamon sugar

Whisk together dry ingredients in a bowl. Chop well-drained apples; add to dry ingredients. Mix together milk, water and vanilla; stir into dry ingredients until well combined. Drop by heaping tablespoons into deep hot oil, 350° F. Fry until golden brown 3-3½ minutes. Drain on paper towels. Roll in cinnamon sugar. Makes 1½-2 dozen.

Trail Mix

Make your own trail mix with raisins, dried apple and banana slices, coconut, nuts and other dried fruit.

Potato Pearls and Freeze-dried Fruits and Vegetables

These make a delicious and nutritious snack.

Sugar Popcorn

1 T. oil
⅓ c. popcorn

2 T. sugar

Heat oil in heavy pan. Add popcorn. After first kernel of popcorn pops, quickly sprinkle sugar over popcorn kernels. Cover and cook over medium heat, shaking pan constantly. Remove pan from heat just before popcorn is finished popping. Sugar will burn easily if you wait for the last kernel to pop.

—Anna Benally

Caramel Popcorn

2½ c. brown sugar, packed
1 (14-oz.) can sweetened condensed milk

1 c. light corn syrup
½ c. butter flavored shortening
popcorn, popped (about 6 quarts)

Combine all ingredients, except popcorn, in saucepan; heat on medium heat stirring constantly until it boils for 1-2 minutes and sugar has dissolved. Pour over popcorn and stir gently. Makes 15 balls, if desired.

—Charlotte Putman

Flavored Gelatin Popcorn Balls

1 c. light corn syrup
1 (3-oz.) pkg. flavored gelatin

1 c. sugar
6 quarts popped popcorn

In saucepan, stir together corn syrup and gelatin. Stir in sugar and heat on low until sugar is dissolved. Pour over popcorn and form into balls.

Fruit Leather

Puree any kind of fruit, bottled (drained) or fresh. (Even old bottled fruit makes great fruit leather.) Add corn syrup as desired to sweeten fresh fruit.

Sun Drying: Prepare a cookie sheet(s) lined with plastic wrap secured in the corners and at the sides with little bits of masking tape. One cookie sheet holds about 2 cups puree. Spread evenly over plastic wrap. Set in sun to dry.

Drinks

Flavored Milk Ideas

Vanilla Nutmeg Milk

Mix:
1 qt. reconstituted dry milk
3 T. sugar
½ t. vanilla
⅛ t. nutmeg
small pinch salt

Maple Sweet Milk

Mix:
1 qt. reconstituted dry milk
⅓ c. corn syrup
½ t. maple flavoring

Sugar 'N Spice Drink Mix

Mix:
2½ c. dry milk
½ c. sugar
¼ salt
½ t. nutmeg

Use 3 to 4 T. of mix to each cup warm or cold water.

Hot Chocolate Drink Mix (great for rotating dry milk)

5 c. powdered milk
3¾ c. sugar

1¼ c. cocoa
1¼ t. salt

Combine above ingredients and store in a #10 can. For hot chocolate, combine ⅓ cup mix in 1 cup hot water. Stir in ¼ t. vanilla.

Amazing Powdered Wassail

2 c. Tang
1½ c. sugar
⅓-½ c. powdered lemon-aid mix

1 t. cinnamon
½ t. ground cloves

Combine ingredients and store in covered container. Mix 1 heaping tablespoon to a mug of hot water; stir and enjoy.

Garden Harvest with Food Storage

The possibilities for using your garden harvest in recipes are endless. Here are a few recipes that get you started combining food storage ingredients with the harvest from your garden.

Main Dishes & Salads

Turkey Zucchini Tetrazzini

1 (10-oz.) can cream of mushroom soup
¾ c. water
¼ c. evaporated milk
¼ c. reconstituted dry milk
¼ c. Parmesan cheese
1 T. dried onion

¾ t. chicken bouillon
1 (10-oz.) can turkey or chicken
1-2 c. sliced zucchini
1½ c. cooked noodles
toasted, sliced almonds (optional)

Combine ingredients in first column and bouillon in a bowl. Lightly toss in remaining ingredients. Pour into greased 1½-quart casserole. Bake at 375° for 30 minutes. Serves 4-5. **Stove Top Method**: Cook zucchini in broth until tender crisp. Combine ingredients in first column. Stir into cooked zucchini and heat on medium until boiling. Add chicken, noodles and almonds and heat through.

Chicken and Broccoli with Noodles

2 pkgs. chicken flavor ramen noodles
1 (10-oz.) can cream of mushroom soup
¾ c. reconstituted dry milk
1 (10-oz.) can chicken, undrained

2 c. broccoli, chopped, cooked
2 T. parsley, chopped
2 tomatoes, cut in big chunks

Cook ramen noodles in 10-inch frying pan according to package directions. Add seasoning packets. Let stand 5 minutes. Drain liquid. Combine soup and milk. Stir into noodles. Lightly toss in rest of ingredients, except tomatoes. Heat through. Toss in tomatoes and serve immediately. Serves 4-5.

Quick Bean Salad

5¼ c. soaked and cooked any dry beans OR
   3 (15-oz.) cans beans, any combination
1 stalk celery, chopped
Dressing:
¼ c. oil
1 T. parsley, chopped
1 t. vinegar
1 T. bottled lemon juice

1 green cucumber, sliced
2 t. sliced green onion

½ t. dry mustard
¼ t. sugar
⅛ t. ground ginger

Mix together beans, celery, cucumber and onion in bowl. Combine dressing ingredients together. Pour over salad; toss until well combined. Chill and serve. Serves 4.

Chicken Lettuce Salad with Honey Dressing

1 (10-oz.) can chicken chunks
1½ c. green or red seedless grapes
1 t. sliced green onion
2 T. green pepper, chopped
Honey Dressing:
¼ c. oil
1 T. honey

2 oranges, peeled and sectioned OR
1 (11-oz.) can mandarin oranges
3 c. lettuce, torn into bite-size pieces

2 t. white vinegar
½ t. salt

Prepare Honey Dressing first. Toss all ingredients, including dressing, together (except oranges and lettuce). Chill for 1 hour. Toss in oranges and lettuce; serve. Serves 4.

Chicken Spinach Salad

½ lb. fresh spinach leaves, washed OR
fresh chard, washed stems removed
and chopped
Vinaigrette Dressing:
¼ c. oil
¼ c. red-wine vinegar
¼ c. juice from mandarin oranges

1-2 (10-oz.) cans chicken chunks, drained
2 c. fresh strawberries, washed, hulled and halved
1 (10-oz.) can mandarin oranges, well-drained

3 T. sugar
¼ t. dry mustard

In a large bowl, combine salad ingredients. Toss to mix. Combine all dressing ingredients immediately before serving and toss with salad. Serves 4-6.

Tuna Spinach Salad

1 (15-oz.) can kidney or garbanzo beans
1 (6-oz.) can tuna, drained
20 spinach leaves or 8 large chard
leaves, stems removed & chopped
Dressing:
⅓ c. oil
2 T. white vinegar or bottled lemon juice

2-3 medium tomatoes, cut in wedges
1 small cucumber, peeled and sliced
1 small red pepper, sliced (optional)
1 c. alfalfa sprouts (optional)

¾ t. sugar
¼ t. dry mustard
⅛ t. salt

Combine dressing ingredients and set aside. Rinse beans; drain well. Combine salad ingredients in large bowl; mix well. Pour dressing over salad just before serving. Serves 4-5.

Side Dish Salads

Coleslaw

½ small cabbage, shredded
2 medium carrots, peeled and grated

2 stalks celery, sliced
1 green onion, finely sliced

Dressing:
½ c. salad dressing (Miracle Whip)

4 t. bottled lemon juice

Combine vegetables in large bowl. Whisk together salad dressing and lemon juice and stir through salad. Serve immediately. Serves 6-8.

Tangy Green Bean and Tomato Salad

2 c. fresh green beans, sliced & cooked
1 fresh tomato, cut in chunks
2 T. olive oil
1 T. wine vinegar

1 T. water
½ t. salt
¼ t. garlic powder
⅛ t. oregano

Put green beans and tomato in bowl. Combine rest of ingredients and pour over salad. Chill, toss and serve. Serves 4.

Curried Rice Salad

2 c. cooked rice
1 red apple, chopped
1 t. green onion, chopped OR
    1 T. chives

¼ c. raisins
2 T. green pepper, chopped

Dressing:
½ c. oil
¼ c. cider vinegar

2 t. brown sugar, packed
½ t. curry powder

Mix dressing ingredients together. Combine salad ingredients together in a bowl. Pour dressing over and toss. Chill for 1 hour. Serves 4-6.

Quick Bread

Garden Harvest Quick Bread

3 c. flour (whole wheat or white)
3 T. dried whole egg, sifted
2 t. cinnamon
1 t. salt
1 t. baking soda
½ t. baking powder

1 c. walnuts, chopped
1½ c. sugar
1 c. oil
6 T. water
1 t. vanilla
2 c. fruit or vegetable (instructions below)

Stir together ingredients in first column. Blend together sugar, oil, water and vanilla and your choice of fruit or vegetables. Stir into flour mixture just until moistened. Pour into greased and floured 4½x8½-inch loaf pans. Bake at 350° F for 50-60 minutes. Let stand 10 minutes before removing from pan. Makes 2 loaves.

Tomato bread: Chop, seed, and peel 3-4 tomatoes and eliminate cinnamon and vanilla.
Zucchini bread: Coarsely shred 2 zucchini to make 2 cups.
Apple bread: Peel and shred 3-4 tart apples to make 2 cups. Mix with 1 t. bottled lemon juice.

Side Dish

Onion Rings

1 c. Super Quick Mix, pg. 53
2 T. cornmeal
1 T. dried whole egg, sifted
1 T. instant dry milk
½ t. dry mustard

¼ t. paprika
⅛ t. cayenne
1 c. water
1-2 fresh onions, sliced
oil

Whisk dry ingredients together; add water and whisk until there are no lumps. Dry sliced onion rings on paper towels. Dip onion rings in batter and fry in hot oil 2-3 minutes turning once.
Variation: Dip and fry other sliced fresh vegetables.

—Tresa Hansen

120

APPENDICES

APPENDIX A

ECONOMICAL STORAGE SPACE AND ROTATING IDEAS

NOTE: It is important to date everything that you store so you can get through your food within its shelf life.

FURNITURE FOR LONG SHELF LIFE FOODS
The following items can be constructed to last a good while. But be aware that you must eventually use and replace the foods stored in this furniture.

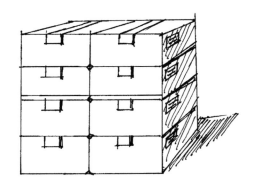

Stacked Boxes (#10 cans) Bedside or Lamp Table
Stack 8 boxes containing 6 #10 cans each; cover with a decorative cloth. (This space holds approximately 300 lbs. of grains - the total amount of grains needed for 1 person for 1 year.)

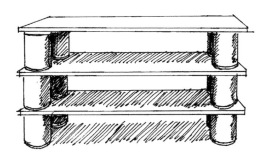

Bookcase
A bookcase can be made with sturdy boards supported on 2 buckets or #10 cans for the supports between each shelf.

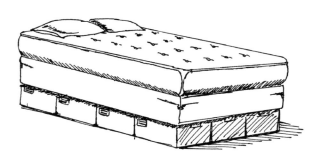

Bed Frames
A box spring can be supported on #10 cans in their boxes or on buckets.

A slippery board placed under boxes or buckets makes it easier to push old ones out and new ones in as needed.

Food Storage Closet

A lot of food storage can be stored in closets, even if you can spare just one closet somewhere in your home.

Closet floor space is also a great place to stack cases or buckets. Look for this extra space in children's closets or in closets where short items are hung.

Rotating System Under a Bed

Make a long cardboard tray from a furniture box (ask at your local furniture store) to fit under a single bed. It should be long enough to reach from one side of the bed to the other and have 4-inch high sides. Place dated canned foods in rows by kind of food in the tray. New dated cans are rolled into to the appropriate row on one side of the bed and older cans are taken from the opposite.

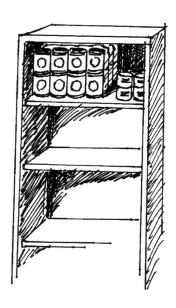

Cans in a Bookcase (idea for small families)

A lot of food storage can be stored in a bookcase. It is ideal to find or build a bookcase with shelves far enough apart to stack two cans high. For maximum storage space, use a tall bookcase where possible.

Use older, dated cans from far left row (front to back) until a full row is emptied. Slide two thin, 3 to 4-inch wide boards on either side of the next row of cans where one can stacks on the other to keep them from tipping. Using the boards, slide cans, one full row at a time, to the left leaving an empty row to fill with new dated cans. Do this in the section for each type of canned food you store in these shelves.

123

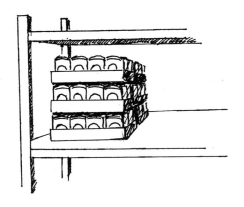

Cans by the Half Case (idea for large families)

On large storage shelves, stack dated half cases of food (in cans smaller than #10 cans) by category as many deep and high as the shelves will permit. Keep the oldest half cases to the top front of each shelf. As half cases are used, add new dated ones to the back and bottom of the category section. If you buy food by the case, it's easier to stack and rotate if you cut the box into half cases.

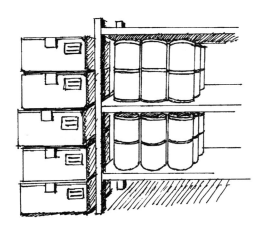

#10 Cans by the Case

When shelf space is limited, cases of dated #10 cans can be stacked floor to ceiling keeping food in categories. To make rotating easy, empty 1 case of each kind of food onto storage shelves, stacking them in rows. Restock your shelves as needed. (This makes 6 cans of each food easily accessible before have to get into your stacks again.) A package of toilet paper or some other soft material can be stuffed between the top box in a stack and the ceiling in an effort to stabilize the stack during earthquake.

- To prevent condensation, boxes, buckets or cans should always be kept off a concrete floor by placing them on wooden pallets, bricks, or some other material. This is a good idea to preserve carpet as well.
- Fashion a lip on the edge of shelves to hold food in place in case of an earthquake. Bottled foods should be stored in boxes with dividers for protection. (Newly canned jars can be returned to their original boxes.)
- If you live in a flood-prone area, store food 3-4 feet off the floor.

APPENDIX B

COOKING WITH STORED FOOD:
CONVERTING FAVORITE RECIPES AND PREPARATION TIPS

The information in this section will help you substitute storable ingredients in place of fresh foods, allowing you to convert your own favorite recipes into food storage recipes.

FOOD STORAGE CONVERSION EQUIVALENTS	
bacon, 5 slices, diced and fried	½ (2-oz.) jar real bacon pieces
broth, 1 cup 1 (14½ -oz.) can	1 t. bouillon granules (or bouillon cube equivalent) + 1 cup water 1¾ t. bouillon granules + 1¾ cup water
buttermilk or sour milk, 1 cup	1 T. vinegar or lemon juice + reconstituted dry or evaporated milk to make 1 cup; let stand 5 minutes
carrots, 1 medium, sliced or diced	¼ c. dried diced carrots + ½ c. water
celery, 1 stalk, sliced	1 T. dried sliced celery + 2 T. water (This small amount of water is not required for a soup or stew.)
beans, dried, 1 (15-oz.) can beans OR 1¾ cup cooked beans	¾ cup dried beans (Sort & rinse. Soak in 2¼ cups water; cook for 1-1 ½ hours.)
egg, 1 whole	1 T. dried whole egg + 2 T. water
garlic, 1 clove	¼-½ t. dried minced garlic OR ⅛ t. garlic powder
green pepper, ¼ cup, diced	2 T. dried, diced green pepper + 2 T. water (This small amount of water is not required for a soup or stew.)
onion, 1 medium, chopped 1 tablespoon, chopped	¼ c. dried onion + ¼ c. water OR 1 t. onion powder 1 t. dried onion OR pinch of onion powder
potatoes, 1 medium, peeled and diced	½ c. dried potato dices + ¾ c. water

© 2003 Probert, Harkness, <u>Emergency Food in a Nutshell</u>, 2nd Edition, Revised

All other dried fruits and vegetables are generally hydrated in double the amount of water.
<u>Dried foods</u> hydrate more quickly in warm to hot water.

    For soups and stews:
- Add dried vegetables and hydrating water with other ingredients. Dried vegetables will hydrate and cook while the soup cooks. Pre-soaking and sauteeing are not necessary.
- Most dried vegetables require a minimum cooking time of 10 minutes. Dried carrots, peas, and

corn require 20-30 minutes.

For salads:

- Green peppers and celery are hydrated in warm tap water for 10-20 minutes while preparing the rest of the recipe. Drain before adding to salad.
- Dried onion does not require hydrating. For best flavor, add dried to salad; let stand 10-20 minutes before serving.
- All other vegetables should be cooked before adding to salad.

Freeze-dried foods hydrate in equal parts water.

- These don't shrink in drying. Double the amount when substituting for dried foods in recipes.
- For soups and stews, add with hydrating water during last 5 minutes of cooking.
- For salads, pre-soak 10-15 minutes in warm tap water; drain and add to salad. (For best flavor, add a little sugar as peas hydrate.)

PREPARATION TIPS

Sanitizing in an Emergency

To minimize the introduction of bacteria during food preparation, thoroughly wash and rinse all dishes, utensils and wash cloths. Sanitize all items in a solution of one teaspoon bleach per one quart warm (not boiling) water and allow to air dry.

Beans/Legumes

- Fast Ideas For Preparing Dried Beans:
    - Overnight Soak: Sort, rinse and soak beans overnight in 3 times water. In the morning, before getting ready for the day, bring beans to boil in soaking water. Reduce heat and simmer, covered, while getting ready, 1-1½ hours. (The darker the bean, the longer they need to cook.) Drain and store in fridge for quick meal preparation at night. Use as canned beans in recipes. **Throwing away soaking and cooking water, reduces problems with gas**.
    - Quick Soak: Sort, rinse and add beans to 3 times water. Bring to boil 2 minutes; allow to sit 1 hour. Then simmer beans, covered, for 1-1½ hours. Drain and use as canned beans in recipes. **Beans cooked this way will produce more problems with gas**.
    - Cook enough beans for more than 1 meal at a time.
      Beans store in fridge 4-5 days; in freezer for up to 6 months.
    - Bottle beans using a pressure canner to make your own canned beans.
    - Store canned beans. These are already cooked. Store 2½ times the quantity of dried beans required. **These beans, when drained, produce the least problems with gas**.
- Acidic substances such as tomatoes, vinegar, wine, etc. slow the softening/cooking of beans. Cook beans in plain water first, then simmer beans with rest of recipe ingredients for 20-30 minutes to blend flavors.
- Hard water increases the time for both soaking and cooking beans. Add ⅛-¼ t. baking soda to cooking water to shorten the cooking time.
- One tablespoon of oil added to beans during cooking reduces foaming and boil overs.
- Cooking old beans:
  Add 1 cup beans and 2 t. baking soda to 3 c. water and soak overnight. Rinse them twice. Put beans in large pot, cover with 1 inch of water and cook about 2 hours, until tender. Add more water if necessary.
- **Reduce gas problems from eating beans by eating them regularly**. Oregon State University says, "by eating a small amount of beans often, your body usually can adjust."

126

Cheese

- Bottled Processed Sharp Cheese Spread is very salty; eliminate or reduce salt in a recipe when adding this cheese to compensate for its high salt content. Melts easily in soups and stews.
- Freeze-dried sharp cheddar cheese has a great flavor and works best when hydrated and sprinkled on top of a dish to be baked. If added to a soup or stew it tends to stick badly on the bottom of the pan. Hydrate 1 c. cheese in ½ c. lukewarm water while preparing a recipe.
- Cheese Powder may be added directly to recipes. Or add Cheese Powder to small amount of water to make a thick cheese paste. If flavor is too strong, combine one part cheese powder with one part flour; whisk in 2 parts water and cook, stirring constantly until thickened. Cook additional 30 seconds to 1 minute to eliminate "floury" taste. This preserves cheese flavor when cheese sauce is added to other ingredients.
- Cheese Sauce Mix contains cheese powder plus white sauce ingredients. It will thicken when added to water and cooked. White sauce ingredients tend to dilute the cheese flavor, resulting in a weaker cheese taste when combined with other foods, even macaroni.
- Cheese Blend usually has blue cheese in it, probably to overcome the problem of flavor loss when combined with other foods. It also has white sauce thickening ingredients.
- Fresh cheese can be frozen. This causes it to become crumbly; grate it before freezing. This is ideal as long as electricity is not cut off during an emergency.

Eggs, Dried Whole

- Dried whole eggs work well in any baked foods—their taste is unnoticeable. Some people do not mind their taste when they are made into scrambled eggs. However, dried egg mix tastes better when scrambled.
- Dried whole eggs are lumpy. They can quickly be sifted by pushing them through a small, fine sieve with the back of the same tablespoon used to measure them.
- Dried whole eggs do not have the same binding quality that fresh eggs do. It is possible to get dried eggs to set in custards, custard-type pies and quiches with double or triple the amount of fresh eggs called for in a recipe. This greatly increases the cholesterol.
- Store-bought cake mixes made with dried eggs are crumbly. The best way to cook a cake mix using dried eggs is to make it into cupcakes. This makes its crumbly texture more manageable.
- Dried egg mix contains dried whole eggs, powdered milk, and other ingredients. It's possible to use it in many recipes in place of dried whole eggs using double the amount. Dried whole eggs are nutritionally closer to using fresh eggs.

Fruit and Vegetables, Canned or Bottled

- The advantage of these foods is that they do not require hydrating time or water.
- Canned foods often contain generous amount of salt. Compensate for this by adding little or no salt to recipes calling for these foods.
- Whenever the recipe says to drain vegetables, save nutrient-filled liquid to put in a soup or stew, or mix with bouillon and make a gravy to serve over bread.
- Drained fruit juice can be consumed by itself or added to a fruit drink mix.
- Because canned foods are already cooked, it's important to avoid heating them excessively so as not to diminish their nutrients.
- Canned tomatoes and pineapple add important vitamin C to any recipe, especially when not overcooked. These ingredients are often simmered with other ingredients to blend flavors in a recipe. During an emergency, when preserving vitamin C is important, it would be best to add these and any other canned foods containing vitamin C last and just heat through even though some flavor will be sacrificed.
- Mash or puree nutritious diced tomatoes to hide them in recipes when chunks are not desired.

Fruits and Vegetables, Dried
- When hydrating fruits and vegetables, the idea is to wind up with as little water as possible to avoid throwing away precious water-soluble vitamins. Use leftover soaking water whenever possible in the recipe.
- Some dried foods like carrots, corn, and peas, take more time to hydrate. Cooking them can speed up the process.
- Home-dried foods can take longer than commercially dried foods to hydrate.
- Use dried foods in a soup or stew by adding them directly to the dish with the required water to hydrate. They are cooked and hydrated at the same time—15-30 minutes, until tender.
- Sauteeing vegetables before adding them to a recipe can be eliminated when using dried vegetables.

Fruits and Vegetables, Freeze-Dried
- When using freeze-dried fruits and vegetables in place of dried, use double the amount of dried.
- Freeze-dried foods hydrate more quickly than dried, and if left to cook for long times, their flavor will weaken in the presence of other ingredients. It is best to add these foods toward the end of the cooking time.
- When eating freeze-dried peas by themselves, add a very small amount of sugar to hydrating water for the fresh taste of frozen peas.

Meats, Canned
- Because canned meats are high in sodium, the amount of salt in recipes using canned meats should be reduced or eliminated.
- Include any extra broth from canned meats into calculations for water added anywhere in the recipe. It can also be saved for soup, stew or gravy.
- To cut cost, 1 (10-12 oz.) can of meat can be substituted for 1½-2 lbs. fresh meat in a recipe.
- Turkey and chicken can be used interchangeably in recipes.
- Add canned turkey, and especially chicken, last in recipes to prevent them from becoming stringy.
- Bottled bacon should be added to a recipe just before serving to preserve its flavor.

Milk, Dried
- To rotate, reconstituted dried milk can be mixed, half and half, with regular milk. Try serving plain reconstituted powdered milk from time to time to get family members used to the taste.
- The flavor of reconstituted dry milk can be improved by adding vanilla or evaporated milk (up to ½ c. per gallon).
- Powdered milk can be added to recipes either reconstituted or as a powder with extra water.
- Shorten cooking time for commercial cooked puddings by heating water instead of milk on high to almost boiling. Lower heat to medium and whisk in pudding mix with enough dry milk to turn the water into milk. Stir only 2-3 minutes until pudding boils and thickens.
- Powdered buttermilk gives the flavor, but not the same leavening quality as real buttermilk.

Milk, Evaporated
- Mixing evaporated milk with an equivalent amount of water makes whole milk.
- Whenever you have evaporated milk leftover from a recipe, mix it with reconstituted dry milk or use in one of the following ways:
  - For a whipped topping, chill and whip, adding sugar and vanilla. (See Evaporated Milk Whipped Topping, pg. 102)
  - For pouring cream, mix with an equal amount of reconstituted dry milk.
  - For sour cream, add 1 T. vinegar or lemon juice to 1 c. undiluted evaporated milk and let stand for 5 minutes.
- Evaporated milk's rich, caramelized flavor enhances the flavor of drinks, casseroles, soups, cooked puddings, creamed rice, pie fillings and frozen desserts.

- To minimize distinctive flavor, scald it when adding to an uncooked dish.

Powdered Butter
- Has a rich flavor when added to recipes but does not taste like fresh butter by itself.
- Less expensive margarine powder can be used in place of butter powder with a sacrifice in flavor.
- Powdered butter makes wonderful white sauce/soup base (*See Super Quick White Sauce Mix, pg. 53*) but does not give good results in cakes and cookies.

Powdered Shortening
- Powdered shortening works well in a quick mix type recipe, but does not give good results in cakes and cookies. It is better to store some regular shortening for these recipes.

TVP
- The flavor of TVP can be enhanced by hydrating it in bouillon. If taco flavored TVP is too spicy, it can be mixed with beef TVP to tone it down. TVP is so easy to substitute in any recipe that we have not included recipes using it.

Wheat
- The fastest way to use wheat is to grind it into flour and use it in place of white flour.
- Another quick way to use your ground wheat flour is to make your own Bisquick® mix. See Super Quick Mix in the index.
- The finer wheat flour is ground, the better it will rise. It is possible, in most recipes, to substitute wheat flour for white flour without any alterations.
- Some recipes work best using half white flour and half whole wheat flour which gives a lighter texture to the end product.
- Most cookie recipes will convert easily to 100% whole wheat if the fat in the recipe is regular shortening. This is a great way to get your family started eating whole wheat.
- Ways to Cook Wheat: (See Recipes, Breakfasts—Cooked Wheat; Thermos Wheat.)

Appendix C

Two Month Menu of Food Storage Meals

See Recipe Section for recipes not included. In an emergency desserts may be an luxury and have not been included in this menu. See dessert section in recipes for ideas. Garden Harvest recipes have also not been included. Make these and other substitutions as soon as harvest begins.

Four Week Menu

Sunday	Monday	Tuesday	Wednesday	Thursday	Friday	Saturday
B: Cream of Wheat L: Canned Soup w/ Biscuits or Toast D: Fabulous Soup Mix Soup/Biscuits	B: Toast & Honey/Jam L: Spanish Rice & Five Bean Salad D: Hawaiian Haystacks	B: Orange Muffins L: Tuna Potato Patties D: Mexican Bean Sauce with Fettuccine/Vegetables	B: Oatmeal L: Chicken Sandwiches D: Beef Barley Stew/Cornbread Muffins	B: French Toast L: Scalloped Potatoes D: Lentil Chili & Flour Tortillas/Vegetables	B: Cracked Wheat Cereal L: Stretch-A-Can of Chili/Navajo Fry Bread D: Tuna Rice Bake/Vegetables	B: Pancakes L: Peanut Butter Sandwiches D: Any Bean Soup with Vegetables
B: Six or Nine Grain Cereal L: Tuna Noodle Salad D: Beef Goulash/Vegetables	B: Toast & Honey/Jam L: Fried Spam Sandwiches D: Split Pea Soup/Rolls	B: Pineapple Muffins L: Fried Potatoes w/ Spam/Bacon D: Salmon Patties/Curried Pasta Salad/Vegetables	B: 6 Grain Cereal L: Warm Mediterranean White Bean Salad D: Fiesta Refried Beans/Corn Salad	B: French Toast L: Quick Potato Soup D: Seven Layered Chicken Casserole/Vegetables	B: Cream of Wheat L: Pinto Bean Wraps D: Lentil Bacon Soup/Cornbread Muffins	B: German Pancakes L: Peanut Butter Sandwiches D: Creamed Meat on Rice/Vegetables
B: Oatmeal L: Canned Soup /Biscuits or Toast D: Pork 'n Beans Baked Beans/Cornbread	B: Toast & Honey/Jam L: Mexicali Bean and Rice Salad D: Corned Beef Hash/Vegetables	B: Apple Muffins L: Vegetable Cheese Soup D: White Bean and Turkey Chili/Vegetables	B: Oatmeal L: Turkey Salad Sandwiches D: Pineapple Chicken/Vegetables	B: French Toast L: Rich Italian Mushroom Sauce & Pasta D: Senate Bean Soup/Biscuits	B: Cracked Wheat Cereal L: Potato Soup D: Turkey Cranberry Pancakes/Vegetables	B: Cornmeal Pancakes L: Peanut Butter Sandwiches D: Savory Indian Lentils/Corn Fritters
B: Cream of Wheat L: White Bean and Bow Tie Salad D: Barbecue Beef Casserole/Vegetables	B: Toast & Honey/Jam L: Tuna Broccoli Soup D: Chili on Spaghetti	B: Oatmeal Muffins L: Fried Rice D: Green Beans and Turkey /Mashed Potatoes or Rice/Vegetables	B: 6 Grain Cereal L: Chicken, Hominy and White Beans D: Lima Bean Soup	B: French Toast L: Pork 'n Beans on Toast D: Swiss Steak with Parsley Potato Mounds/Vegetables	B: Cream of Wheat L: Spam and Pasta Salad D: Vegetarian Chili/Hush Puppies	B: Pancakes L: Peanut Butter Sandwiches D: Curry Beef on Rice/Vegetables

130

Five Week Menu

	Sunday	Monday	Tuesday	Wednesday	Thursday	Friday	Saturday
	B: Oatmeal L: Can Soup/ Biscuits or Toast D: Zippy Quick Baked Beans/Biscuits	B: Toast & Honey/Jam L: Fried Spam Sandwiches D: Chicken or Turkey Crepes/Vegetables	B: Pineapple Muffins L: Tuna Potato Patties D: Split Pea Stew/Muffins	B: Oatmeal L: Tuna Salad Sandwiches D: Creamy Chicken & Green Beans/ Mashed Potatoes	B: French Toast L: Scalloped Potatoes D: Quick Beef Chili and Corn /Cornbread	B: Cracked Wheat Cereal L: Tuna on Rice D: Beef or Chicken and Bean Enchiladas/Corn Salad	B: German Pancakes L: Peanut Butter Sandwiches D: Simply Delicious Beans/Rolls
	B: Cream of Wheat L: Creamy Red Beans and Pasta Salad D: Croquettes/ Vegetables	B: Toast & Honey/Jam L: Spanish Rice & Five Bean Salad D: Spamtastic Pork 'N Beans/ Vegetables	B: Apple Muffins L: Fried Potatoes D: Southwestern Chicken or Turkey Barley Soup/Muffins	B: 6 Grain Cereal L: Chicken Noodle Salad D: Cheesy Beans & Rice/Vegetables	B: French Toast L: Tomato Risotto D: Meat and Gravy on Mashed Potatoes OR Salmon Loaf/ Vegetables	B: Cream of Wheat L: Stretch-A-Can of Chili & Navajo Fry Bread D: Buckaroo Beans	B: Cornmeal Pancakes L: Peanut Butter Sandwiches D: Chicken 'n' Dumplings
	B: Six or Nine Grain Cereal L: Can Soup with Biscuits/Toast D: Bean and Bacon Hot Pot/Biscuits	B: Toast & Honey/Jam L: Corn Chowder D: Sweet & Sour Beef/Rice	B: Orange Muffins L: Rich Italian Mushroom Sauce & Pasta D: Minestrone/ Cornbread	B: Oatmeal L: Chicken/Turkey/ Tuna Salad Sandwiches D: Lasagne/ Vegetables	B: French Toast L: Quick Potato Soup D: Ham and Bean Soup/Rolls	B: Cracked Wheat Cereal L: Pork 'n Beans on Toast D: Mushroom Chicken and Noodles/ Vegetables	B: Pancakes L: Peanut Butter Sandwiches D: Puerto Rican Black Beans and Rice/Corn Salad
	B: Oatmeal L: Hawaiian Bean Salad D: Tuna Mornay/ Vegetables	B: Toast & Honey/Jam L: Creamy Broccoli Rice Soup D: Mexican White Bean and Turkey Chowder	B: Oatmeal Muffins L: Plain Pinto Beans w/ Pickle Relish & Yummy Potato Salad D: Salmon Chowder/ Cornbread	B: 6 Grain Cereal L: Chicken/Turkey/ Tuna Salad Sandwiches D: Santa Fe Lentils/Flour Tortillas	B: French Toast L: New England Clam Chowder D: Beef Stew/Biscuits	B: Cream of Wheat L: Potato Soup D: Bean and Lentil Rice Pilaf/ Vegetables	B: German Pancakes L: Peanut Butter Sandwiches D: Chicken Corn Soup/Cornbread Muffins
	B: Cream of Wheat L: Can Soup with Biscuits/Toast D: Pinto Beef Tamale Pie OR Tamales/ Vegetables	B: Toast & Honey/Jam L: Complete-meal Tuna Helper D: Corned Beef with Parsley Sauce/ Vegetables	B: Apple Muffins L: Broccoli Soup D: Lentil Stew or Lentil Vegetable Soup/Corn Fritters	B: Oatmeal L: Italian Chicken and Bean Soup D: Fettuccine Carbonara/ Vegetables	B: French Toast L: Tomato Risotto D: Red Beans and Rice/Cornbread	B: Cracked Wheat Cereal L: Spanish Rice D: Country Meat Pie/Vegetables	B: Cornmeal Pancakes L: Peanut Butter Sandwiches D: Eureka Kidney Bean Soup/Biscuits

APPENDIX D

FUEL OPTIONS: SAFETY, STORAGE AND COOKING METHODS

To be truly prepared, you will need to plan for alternative cooking methods in case normal energy sources are disrupted. Alternative cooking methods require the use and storage of fuels. **Safety is the prime consideration in deciding what you will store and use.** The information in this appendix will help you decide which cooking methods and fuels will work best for you. Before making any decisions, it is important to thoroughly read through all the information in both the indoor and outdoor cooking sections below. We have explored only the most common fuels for long term use.

The following material has been carefully researched. It is a compilation of information obtained from fuel and appliance industry associations, government safety organizations, and testing/certifying laboratories. Sources for this information can be found at the end of the Outdoor Cooking section.

INDOOR COOKING/HEATING

The primary concern with cooking/heating indoors is carbon monoxide (CO) poisoning. Carbon monoxide is an odorless, poisonous gas that replaces oxygen in the bloodstream causing suffocation. Exposure to high levels of CO can cause headaches, dizziness, weakness, nausea, and confusion quickly leading to unconsciousness and death. Even low levels can cause fatigue and flu-like symptoms and over a long period of time can produce effects similar to high concentrations. According to the U.S. Consumer Product Safety Commission, CO poisoning is responsible for the treatment of nearly 5,000 people in hospital emergency rooms and 300 deaths each year.

All fuels require oxygen to burn efficiently and give off some carbon monoxide. Without a source of fresh oxygen, burning any fuel inside an enclosed area (homes-including basements, mobile homes, garages, sheds, motor homes, vans and tents) reduces available oxygen causing incomplete fuel combustion. Incomplete combustion produces dangerous amounts of carbon monoxide. Therefore, adequate ventilation must be provided at all times to ensure complete fuel combustion.

Indoor cooking/heating appliances fall into two general categories:
   –Vented appliances have a duct, pipe, chimney or other device to carry pollutants from fuel combustion to the outside of the dwelling.
   –Unvented appliances have no such connection to the outside and release combustion pollutants directly into the inside air. It is wise to choose vented appliances whenever possible.

Information about alternative cooking methods and associated fuels also applies to heating concerns. Keep in mind that fuel is used most efficiently if, when heating, you can cook from the same source.

GENERAL SAFETY GUIDELINES
   ▸ Be sure to check with your local fire authorities to see what cooking/heating devices and fuels you can legally use and store in your community. Also check your insurance policy, rental contract, or building regulations for any restrictions.
   ▸ It is critical that fuels (whatever kind you decide to store) be stored in legal amounts allowed by local fire and city or county authorities. Storing more than legal amounts endangers not only your life and property but also that of you neighbors. It also endangers the life of any member of the fire department called to a fire on your property. Additionally, you could be fined and nullify your insurance policy.

132

- The only combustion appliances safe to use inside are those that have been tested and certified for indoor use. Certified appliances will bear a label or some other mark of certification. Reputable certifying organizations include:
   Underwriters Laboratories (UL)
   American Gas Association (AGA) or Canadian Standards Association (CSA) which are the same
   Environmental Protection Agency (EPA) for wood stoves
- Beware of product advertisements or literature claiming that any burning fuel gives off only harmless carbon dioxide (CO^2) making it completely safe to use inside. All burning fuels give off some amounts of carbon monoxide (CO), and in oxygen depleted environments (enclosed areas) CO is produced in large, deadly amounts.
- Because of varying conditions which exist worldwide, it cannot be assumed that the way in which fuels are burned indoors to cook/heat in other countries is necessarily safe in your own home. Newer, airtight or older, winterized homes can develop an oxygen deprived environment rapidly as fuel is burned and the available oxygen is consumed. As explained above, oxygen depleted environments cause burning fuels to produce dangerous amounts of CO.
- Always follow manufacturer's directions in installing, operating, and maintaining your cooking/heating appliance. Never repair an appliance yourself; contact a service representative.
- Never use any fuel in an appliance that is not recommended by the manufacturer. The wrong fuel can burn hotter than the appliance is designed for and can cause a serious fire.
- While using an unvented fuel-burning cooker/heater, open a door to the rest of the house from the room where the appliance is in use AND open an outside window at least an inch to assure adequate ventilation. **Never use this type of unvented heater overnight or in a room where occupants are sleeping**. As available oxygen diminishes and CO concentrations build, occupants will not awaken and will die.
- Never leave a cooker/heater or stove on or a roaring fire in a fireplace. Unattended cooking is the leading cause of home fires in the United States. So, stand by your pan!
- All Boy Scouts know—"No flames in tents." This includes operating a propane or kerosene heater or cooker. Not only is there the danger of starting the tent or belongings on fire but also the serious risk of CO poisoning and death, as has been known to happen.
- Never use a cooker/heater in areas where flammable vapors from gasoline, propane, paint thinners or removers or other solvents are present. The flame of even a match used to light the appliance can cause an explosion or fire.
- Keep bedding, furniture, curtains, wood, newspapers, etc. at least 3 feet away from heater/cookers, wood/coal stoves, and fireplaces. It is a fire hazard to dry clothes too close to a heat source.
- Keep children and pets away from fuel-burning appliances. Don't allow children to tamper or play with fuel containers or appliances even when they're turned off. Also, don't allow children to buy fuel, refuel or operate appliances without supervision.
- According to the Uniform Fire Code, all fuels should be stored away from sources of heat, flame or sparks. Combustible liquid fuels should never be stored in basements.
- Keep a functioning battery-operated smoke detector on each level of your home AND a battery operated carbon monoxide detector close to sleeping areas. Follow manufacturer's instructions carefully for replacing the alarm and/or its battery. However, preventing CO build up in your home is better than relying solely upon an alarm.
- Be sure to have an A/B/C rated fire extinguisher readily available where fuels are stored and used. Follow manufacturer's maintenance instructions to be sure its in working order.
- Have your cooking/heating device checked annually by a trained service representative. This includes wood and coal-burning stoves. Potential problems with these stoves that can only be detected by a professional are a cracked heat exchanger or an insufficient air supply for the fuel to burn properly.

Wood

Safety:
- Read General Safety Guidelines pg. 132.
- When wood is burned indoors it is important that it is vented to the outside due to the large amounts of pollutants and smoke it gives off. It is also necessary to crack a window in newer, air-tight or older, winterized homes so there is enough oxygen in the room for the fuel to burn completely. This also prevents a reverse draft which can suck carbon monoxide fumes into a dwelling.
- All new wood stoves (built after 1992) must be built according to strict EPA regulations which require low pollution emissions.
- Don't burn coal in a wood stove. Coal combusts at a different rate than wood. The supply of oxygen in new wood stoves is not adequate for coal combustion and may result in an explosion of unburned gasses. Over time, the high heat of burning coal can weaken the steel of a wood stove.
- Use aged (dried) hardwoods (oak, elm, maple) which burn hotter and form less creosote. (Creosote is a black, oily, tar-like substance that builds up on the inside of chimneys and stove pipes. When allowed to build up, creosote can ignite and start a fire.) Hard wood burns longer, making it a better option to store. Do not burn large amounts of softwoods (pine, fir, cedar), green or wet wood which create more creosote. Softwoods also burn more quickly.
- Never burn painted or treated wood, plastics, charcoal, or colored newspaper (comics) because of the highly toxic pollutants they release. Burning trash, charcoal, or plastics in a wood-burning device can cause it (and/or the chimney) to overheat and catch on fire. Burning paper or pine boughs can send ignited particles floating up a chimney and to the outside where they can start a fire. Pay close attention to burning instructions for compressed wood or wood wax logs given by manufacturers.
- Never use charcoal lighter fluid or kerosene to start a fire in your stove or fireplace. Small amounts of softwoods work well to start hardwood fires.
- Before opening a stove door to look at the fire or to add wood, open the stove damper. This sends both pollutants and gasses up the chimney, preventing them from being drawn into the room. Additionally, this eliminates the possibility of flare-up when air suddenly enters in through the door.
- When using an open fireplace, always use a sturdy fireplace screen to prevent flying embers from starting a fire.
- To keep a fire alive at night or while you are away, bank the fire with ashes or damper it way down.
- Make sure the stove door is tight fitting to prevent the escape of pollutants into your dwelling. Any warped or worn gasket should be replaced. Check door gaskets annually by shutting the door on a dollar bill. If the bill pulls out easily at any place around the door, a new gasket is needed.
- Have a qualified person check chimney for rust and creosote build-up yearly, preferably at the start of heating season. Most fires associated with wood heating appliances occur in the chimney from poorly installed or damaged chimneys, or ignition of creosote. Chimneys that are blocked, leak, or are otherwise damaged can also allow fatal concentrations of carbon monoxide to build up in your dwelling.

Storage:
- Wood is best stored under cover in a convenient outside location. Stack it on a supporting base to keep it away from ground moisture, to allow air to circulate through it, and to reduce insect and dirt accumulation. A standard cord of wood measures approximately 8 ft. long, 4 ft. wide and 4 ft. high. Braces or stakes on the ends of the pile prevent it from collapsing.

- Green wood will season in about 6 months if stored outdoors in a dry, sunny location with good air circulation. Wood becomes seasoned or dry enough to support efficient combustion when the moisture content in the wood equalizes with the moisture in the surrounding air.

Shelf Life:
- Wood will store a very long time as long as it is kept dry.

Possible Cooking Devices and Options:
- EPA-certified woodstoves use fuel most efficiently and produce a minimum of pollutants. One-pot cooking is possible.
- EPA-exempt cookstoves and woodstoves burn fuel fast and produce more pollutants. They can be illegal to use in your area—check with your local authorities. These are good for one-pot cooking and possibly oven baking.
- Open fireplaces consume fuel fast. Dutch Oven and reflector oven cooking are possible.
- A pellet stove is not a good alternative means of cooking because electricity is needed to feed pellets into the stove.

Coal

Safety:
- Read General Safety Guidelines pg. 132.
- When coal is burned indoors, it is important that it is vented to the outside due to the large amounts of pollutants and smoke it gives off. It is also necessary to crack a window in newer, airtight or older, winterized homes so there is enough oxygen in the room for the fuels to burn completely. This also prevents a reverse draft which can suck carbon monoxide fumes into a dwelling.
- Coal stoves are not currently regulated by the EPA. Check with your local environmental air quality authority for regulations regarding the use of coal stoves in your area.
- Only two types of coal are recommended for coal stoves—anthracite and bituminous. Anthracite is harder and burns hotter and cleaner with fewer clinkers while bituminous is soft, produces more soot and smoke and is dirtier to handle.
- Wood can be burned in a coal stove, however, the emissions will be higher than from an EPA approved wood stove.
- Don't burn coal in a wood stove. Coal combusts at a different rate than wood. The supply of oxygen in new wood stoves is not adequate for coal combustion and may result in an explosion of unburned gasses. Over time, the high heat of burning coal can weaken the steel of a wood stove.
- Never use charcoal lighter fluid or kerosene to start coal in a stove. Small amounts of softwoods work well to start coal fires.
- When adding coal to a stove, open the stove damper. This sends both pollutants and gasses up the chimney, preventing them from being drawn into the room. Additionally, this eliminates the possibility of flare-up when air suddenly enters in through the door.
- Make sure the stove door is tight fitting to prevent the escape of pollutants into your dwelling. Any warped or worn gasket should be replaced. Check door gaskets annually by shutting the door on a dollar bill. If the bill pulls out easily at any place around the door, a new gasket is needed.

Storage:
- Coal should be stored in a dry place free of any other combustible materials. Anthracite can be stored outside in the weather. It is unaffected by heat, water, snow and freezing temperatures. Bituminous coal breaks down when exposed to the elements and must therefore be stored in a waterproof bin or shed. A container 4 ft. square and 4 ft. high holds approximately 2 tons of coal.

Shelf Life: ▸ Coal — Anthracite stores indefinitely.
— Bituminous disintegrates over time in less than ideal storage conditions. In ideal conditions, it will last many years.

Possible Cooking Devices and Options:
▸ Coal stoves use fuel efficiently. Stove top cooking is possible.

Kerosene

Safety: ▸ Read General Safety Guidelines pg. 132.
▸ Use only 1K kerosene in your appliance. High-quality kerosene allows the wick to burn properly keeping pollutants and odor to a minimum. Never use kerosene that is cloudy or slightly colored as these indicate the presence of impurities which cause low flame, smoking and odor.
▸ In case of flare-up or uncontrolled flaming, turn the appliance off rather than attempt to move it.
▸ Never refuel your kerosene appliance inside a dwelling. Allow appliance to cool at least 15 minutes before removing heater/cooker or removable fuel tank to the outside for refilling.
▸ Use your appliance until the kerosene tank is empty before storing away for the summer.

Storage: ▸ Store only 1K kerosene. This high-quality kerosene is clear and colorless and has no unusual odors
▸ Store only in clean, opaque, plastic or metal containers approved for fuel storage. To avoid unintentional use of the wrong fuel, make sure all containers are clearly labeled or use color-coded containers (kerosene containers are usually blue, gasoline containers are usually red). Never put kerosene into a container that has been used for other fuels or liquids.
▸ Do not transport kerosene in a plastic container in a plastic bed liner of a truck. The two plastics can create a static spark and cause an explosion.
▸ Store kerosene containers out of sunlight. Heat expedites kerosene breakdown. If local regulations allow, kerosene can be safely stored in a garage or shed. NEVER store kerosene in your basement!
▸ Keep kerosene containers well sealed to prevent moisture from getting into container. Moisture causes the breakdown of kerosene.

Shelf Life: ▸ It is ideal to use the kerosene you store within 1 year. Poor-quality kerosene will usually not keep for longer than a year. If you have stored high-quality kerosene in a well sealed, clean container out of sunlight, it can still be used for up to 3 years. Additives can extend kerosene shelf life. If you decide to use one, be sure to choose a reputable one. Keep in mind that you can use additives for only so long.
▸ When kerosene is past its shelf life, it is necessary to dispose of it following your county environmental safety guidelines. Contact your county officials for information.

Possible Cooking Devices and Options:
▸ Kerosene cooker-heaters are good for one-pot cooking. Look for new ones that shut off automatically if they are tipped or bumped.

136

Propane

Safety:
- Read General Safety Guidelines pg. 132.
- NEVER use a propane appliance intended for outdoor use inside a dwelling, trailer, garage, tent or any other enclosed area. Appliances intended for outdoor use emit large amounts of deadly carbon monoxide as propane is burned.
- A natural gas appliance can be adapted for propane use. However, the gas orifice must be changed to one designed to burn propane. Without this change, the propane will burn incompletely producing dangerous levels of CO.
- Propane appliances intended for indoor use (range, water heater, furnace) and those that have been adapted for indoor propane use (natural gas range fitted for propane) must **always** be connected to a propane source that is **outside**. Propane containers are designed to allow volatile gases to escape through a pressure relief valve making indoor storage and use extremely dangerous. These gases can explode or burn with any source of ignition, even a spark. In the case of an indoor fire, a propane cylinder is like a bomb waiting to go off.
- Never use a propane fitted oven/range to heat your home.
- Unvented indoor propane appliances (like a space heater) should have an oxygen depletion sensor (ODS). This monitors the level of oxygen needed for the fuel to burn efficiently and will automatically shut off the appliance should the oxygen level get too low. Remember, low oxygen environments cause burning fuels to give off dangerous levels of CO. Older appliances do not have an ODS and should be replaced with ones that do. Vented propane appliances do not need an ODS as long as they are installed properly.
- If you smell a persistent or strong odor of gas around your tank, cylinder, or appliance, do not try to light appliance. Extinguish any source of ignition or flame, get everyone out of your dwelling, shut off gas supply at container, and call your gas supplier from a neighbors phone. (After hours, call fire department.) Propane has a rotten egg smell.
- Do not use a propane container that is dented, gouged, bulged or is otherwise damaged. Do not attempt to repair a cylinder in any way; this must be done by your gas supplier.

Storage:
- Store propane containers outside in a location that receives as little direct sunlight as possible. Propane containers have a pressure relief valve which allows for the expansion and escape of volatile gases. Where heat from direct sunlight does not harm propane, heat can cause it to escape wastefully into the air.
- NEVER store propane containers, including the 1-pound cylinders, inside homes (including basements), other dwellings, garages, storage units or sheds, even partially enclosed patios or decks. Never leave containers in a vehicle. Propane is heavier than air and will collect in low places. If it comes in contact with a source of ignition, it will burn or explode. Even a light switch can cause ignition.
- Use only a reputable propane supplier who will be experienced in purging, filling, or testing cylinders or in disposing of unused propane. Brand new cylinders will need to be purged of air and water before filling. Purging is essential to prevent odor fade and improper fuel combustion.
- Propane needs to have space inside the container to expand. Overfilling a container is so dangerous that only a reputable supplier is experienced enough to monitor both the spitter valve and the Overfill Protection Device (OPD), ensuring a safe level of propane inside the container. Old containers that do not have an OPD will be required by law to have one by April 1, 2002.
- Cylinders have a manufacture date stamped on the collar. They need to be recertified 12 years from that date and every 10 years thereafter. Use only a reputable propane supplier who will be experienced in performing the required safety inspections and recertifications.

> ► Cylinders should always be stored and transported in a secured upright position. The pressure relief valve can allow liquid propane to escape if a cylinder is tipped on its side.
> ► Caution: The pressure relief valve will also release propane if a cylinder is left in a hot car. Even opening a trunk with a key can create a spark and cause an explosion. Filled propane tanks, transported in a car, must be taken to a destination and unloaded quickly to prevent a problem.

Shelf Life: ► Indefinite

Possible Cooking Devices and Options:
> ► Propane-converted natural gas ranges are good for stove top and oven cooking.
> ► Propane-fueled imitation wood stoves make stove top cooking possible.
> ► Propane-fueled generators allow for use of some/all household cooking appliances, making a variety of cooking methods possible. (See information below on generators.)
> ► We are not aware of any portable propane appliances that can be used for cooking inside a dwelling. There are, however, propane heaters - look for new ones that have an Oxygen Depletion Sensor (ODS).

Gasoline

Safety: ► Gasoline can NEVER be burned inside a dwelling. In the limited oxygen environment of a dwelling, burning gasoline gives off large amounts of dangerous CO. This information on gasoline has been included for those interested in generators.
> ► Always place a fuel container on the ground before filling with gasoline, preventing fumes or spills from going into your vehicle. Fill it slowly to prevent spills. Having the container on the ground as well as keeping the fuel nozzle in contact with the container during filling, prevents the buildup of a static charge while the container is being filled.
> ► When transporting gasoline, make sure container caps are tight, wipe any fuel off the outside, and secure container in an upright position. Never leave containers, with any amount of gasoline, in a car trunk on a hot day or in direct sunlight.

Storage: ► Store only in a UL approved container. Fire prevention codes strictly prohibit storing gasoline in other containers. UL approved containers will clearly bare a UL marking.
> ► Gasoline must be stored away from any source of ignition (includes: pilot lights of appliances, flames or sparks). Gasoline vapors are heavier than air and can travel along the floor therefore, store and handle gasoline 50 feet away from ignition sources.
> ► Must NOT be stored inside a dwelling, basement, or attached garage. It gives off large amounts of volatile gasses which are dangerous to breathe and can ignite with just a spark. The safest place to store gasoline is in a location separate from a dwelling, such as a shed or unattached garage.
> ► Store gasoline in a cool, well-ventilated location away from moisture that could corrode a metal container or facilitate bacterial growth. If the container or gas tank has to be in direct sunlight or will be stored at temperatures above 80° F most of the time, a fuel stabilizer should be added before storing. Stabilizers prevent the development of gum in the gasoline, bacterial growth, and formation of rust and corrosion on the container.

Shelf Life: ► According to Chevron, gasoline will keep for at least 1 year if it is stored in a cool place in a tightly closed container.

Possible Cooking Devices and Options:
> ► Gasoline-fueled generators allow for use of some/all household appliances, making a variety of cooking methods possible. (See following information on generators.)

A Word About Generators

Generators can be fueled by gasoline, propane, diesel, and natural gas. The least expensive ones are portable. Be aware that generators consume a large amount of fuel, and the length of time they can be used in an emergency is limited to the amount of fuel you can legally store. Use of a generator, even intermittently throughout the day, over a three-day to two-week period of time can require more fuel than is legally allowed for storage in most cities.

Should you decide to use a generator, it can be used in one of two ways. The easier way is to plug appliances directly into the generator. The other way is to connect the generator to the house wiring system. This would not only supply portable appliances, but also those hardwired into the house. If the generator is supplying energy to the house wiring system during an outage, it is **critical** that the connection to the public energy supply be turned off. In a power outage, other homes will draw energy from any power source on the line. This can overwork your generator causing severe damage. If you are not disconnected from the public line, there is also the possibility of a utility worker or someone else being electrocuted from the power your generator is supplying to the public line.

If your home is not already equipped with a transfer switch (not the main circuit breaker) to disconnect the public supply, you will need to have one installed by a licensed electrician **before an emergency**. Be very familiar with all instructions for safe installation and use of your generator before you need to use it.

OUTDOOR COOKING

Safety is still the primary concern when cooking outdoors. This section includes information for fuel usage outside a dwelling or enclosure.

GENERAL SAFETY GUIDELINES:
- ▸ Keep a fire extinguisher, pot of water, shovel, or bucket of sand close to the fire for emergency use.
- ▸ Never leave a fire or ignited propane appliance unattended. Be sure to extinguish all coals and flames before leaving the cooking site.

MOST COMMON OUTDOOR COOKING/HEATING OPTIONS
Wood
Safety:
- ▸ Never burn wood in an enclosed area such as an enclosed a patio, garage, or tent. Breathing smoke and pollutants is harmful and the buildup of carbon monoxide could be deadly.
- ▸ Always burn wood on bare ground away from buildings, trees, bushes, dry grasses or anything else that may catch fire. Also, clear the ground in a 10-foot circle around the fire site of anything that would catch fire from a burning ember. Always watch for wind-blown sparks that could start other fires.
- ▸ Never start fires with gasoline, kerosene, or other volatile fluids which can explode.
- ▸ To conserve fuel, build a fire just big enough for your needs. Large fires are hard to control and to work over. Open flames are good for quick, high-heat cooking while hot coals are good for cooking that requires temperature control.
- ▸ Be prepared to use heavy duty, long handled cooking utensils and pans.

Storage:
- ▸ See Wood—Storage pg. 134 in the Indoor Cooking/Heating Options.

Shelf Life:
- ▸ A very, very long time if kept dry.

Possible Cooking Options:
- ▸ Open flame cooking is good for one-pot cooking.
- ▸ Cooking with coals gives temperature control. This is good for slow cooking, frying, and Dutch Oven cooking. Pit cooking is done by burying a Dutch Oven with coals. This conserves fuel, and is great for cooking dried bean dishes which take longer.
- ▸ For more ideas look for books or manuals that describe outdoor cooking using wood.

Propane

Safety:
- NEVER use a propane appliance intended for outdoor use inside an enclosed area such as a trailer, garage or tent. Appliances intended for outdoor use emit large amounts of deadly carbon monoxide as propane is burned.
- Use your propane appliance in an open place away from buildings, dry leaves or brush.
- Be sure to follow ALL manufacturers instructions for operation, care, and replacement of appliance parts. Never repair an appliance yourself; contact a service representative.
- If you smell a persistent or strong odor of gas around your tank, cylinder, or appliance, do not try to light appliance. Shut off gas supply at container, and have your appliance checked. Propane has a rotten egg smell.
- Do not use a propane container that is dented, gouged, bulged or is otherwise damaged. Do not attempt to repair a cylinder in any way; this must be done by your gas supplier.

Storage:
- See Propane—Storage pg.137 in the Indoor Cooking/Heating Options.
- If you bring your propane appliance inside out of inclement weather, disconnect it first from the propane cylinder which **must always be left outside**. The pressure relief valve continues to allow propane to escape even when connected to an unlit appliance.

Shelf Life:
- Indefinite

Possible Cooking Devices and Options:
- Portable camp stoves or single burners are good for one-pot cooking.
- Gas grills or barbecues are good for one-pot and oven cooking.

Charcoal

Safety:
- NEVER burn charcoal inside an enclosed area such as a camper, tent, van, garage or any dwelling. Charcoal smolders as it burns and gives off very high levels of deadly carbon monoxide. Not even an open window or operating fan are an assurance that carbon monoxide is reduced to safe levels. 25 people die and hundreds suffer the effects of carbon monoxide poisoning by burning charcoal in an enclosed area each year.
- A metal chimney charcoal starter is a simple alternative to storing large amounts of volatile lighter fluid. (One that has small holes going up the sides in addition to the usual large holes around the base is most efficient.) This will start charcoal briquets with the use of newspaper and matches. A supply of newspaper is easily and safely stored.
- Never use gasoline, kerosene, or other explosive fluids to start a fire. Never add lighter fluid to hot/warm coals.
- Charcoal burns without a flame. Once ignited, it begins to turn white. Do not touch to see if it is hot. It takes about 5-10 minutes to reach cooking heat.
- Before disposing, let coals completely burn out and allow the ashes to cool until cold. Dispose of cold ashes in a non-combustible container or in a fire pit. If you must dispose of ashes before they are cold, douse them completely with water. **OR** to conserve fuel, once you are finished cooking, dump charcoals in a bucket of water to extinguish. Immediately drain and spread them on the ground where their residual heat will dry them out so they can be used again for the next meal.

Storage:
- Charcoal <u>must</u> be protected against moisture. The Kingsford Charcoal company says charcoal left in the original paper packaging can be stored in containers lined with garbage bags in a garage or shed. Consult local authorities for safeguards against spontaneous charcoal combustion.
- 1 lb. charcoal = about 15 briquettes.

Shelf Life:
- Indefinite, if kept away from moisture.

Possible Cooking Devices and Options:
- Charcoal coals are good for Dutch Oven and one-pot cooking.
- Applebox Reflector Ovens are great for baking. (See instructions below.)
- For more information, consult books or manuals on outdoor cooking with charcoal.

140

SOURCES :

    American Petroleum Institute
    Barbecue Industry Association
    Blaschak Coal Corporation, Mahandy, Pennsylvania
    Boy Scouts of America
    California Energy Commission
    Kingsford Charcoal Company
    Magic Sweep Corporation, Chesapeake, Virginia
    Michigan State University Extension
    NFPA (National Fire Prevention Association)
    National Kerosene Heater Association
    National Propane Gas Association
    Oakland County, Michigan Health Department
    Provo City Fire Department, Office of Fire Prevention
    SAREC (Science of Anticipation, Recognition, Evaluation, Control of Health Risks Inc.),
        Montreal, Canada
    Snohomish Public Utility District, Everett, Washington
    Sure Appliance, Provo, Utah
    U.S. Consumer Product Safety Commission
    U.S. Environmental Protection Agency

EASY FUEL-SAVING COOKING METHODS:

Haybox Cooking (Cooking with Stored Heat)

This method of cooking uses a small amount of fuel, like propane or other LP gas, to get food cooking. Food then finishes cooking in an insulated container. In World War II times a box filled with hay was used.

<u>Supplies Needed</u>:   A pot

Sturdy container:

    Option 1- A large camping cooler can be used for a "haybox" with only 1-2 inches of insulation around the pot; any less poses the risk of melting the cooler. It doesn't need to be lined.

    Option 2- A container that is at least 4-inches larger on all sides than your pot (cardboard box i.e., computer box, wooden box, plastic or metal garbage can, large metal tub). This container will need to be lined with flannel, heavy fleece, felt or several layers of newspaper.

Insulation material (blankets, shredded newspaper, towels, or any other clean, dry material like hay, straw or sawdust)

Cushion or pillow

Lid or piece of wood to top the container

<u>Cooking Steps</u>:

1. Line container, if needed
2. Fill with insulation material.
3. Make a nest in insulation for the pot, allowing insulation space between pot and container as described in container options above.
4. Assemble food in pot. Food should fill pot ½-⅔ full. Cover and bring to a rolling boil; simmer on medium for 3 minutes.
5. Place piping hot, covered pot into the insulated nest and top with a cushion or pillow. Cover entire container tightly with a lid or piece of wood.

6. Food will take <u>4 times</u> the recommended recipe time to cook. Food will need to be finished cooking within 4-6 hours, depending on how long your haybox will maintain the minimum safe temperature (see CAUTION below). If food needs to be cooked for a longer time, remove pot from the box, bring it to a boil again and return it to the box for the remainder of the cooking time. Examples:

	Usual Cooking Time	"Haybox" Cooking Time
Bean and Bacon Hot Pot	15 min.	1 hour
Rice, long grain	20	1 hour*
Beef Stew	20 min.	1 hr. 20 min.
Lentil Vegetable Soup	45 min.	3 hours
Split Pea Soup	1 hour	4 hours
Cooking Soaked Dry Beans	1-1½ hours	4-6 hours

*Rice doesn't require 4 times the usual cooking time.

7. After required cooking time, remove pot from container and serve. Leave haybox lid open for moisture to evaporate before storing.

<u>This method of cooking is recommended for dishes containing dried legumes and vegetables, canned foods or small chunks of fresh meat.</u>

CAUTION: For safety, food MUST be held above 140° F during the time it is in the container (This is the FDA standard for food safety in restaurants). Test your "haybox" using a pot of boiling water, ½-⅔ full. After 4 hours, remove pot and check temperature with a thermometer. If temperature is too low, add more insulation to your "haybox" and test again.

<u>Test the accuracy of your thermometer</u>, by placing your thermometer in a pot of boiling water for 10 min. to see what temperature it registers. If your thermometer registers higher than the temperature given below for your altitude, <u>add</u> the difference to 140° F for the <u>minimum temperature</u> you must maintain in your "haybox" for safety. If it registers lower, <u>subtract</u> the difference from 140° F.

Altitude Chart (Boiling Point lowers with altitude.)

Sea Level	212° F	4,000 ft.	204.8° F
1,000 ft.	210.2° F	5,000 ft.	203° F
2,000 ft.	208.4° F	7,500 ft.	198.4° F
3,000 ft.	206.6° F	10,000 ft.	194° F

CAUTION: If haybox is stored at very cold temperatures (garage), bring it to room temperature before using.

Applebox Reflector Oven

This is an inexpensive way to prepare any baked foods in an emergency. It uses almost half the charcoal as Dutch oven baking, and gives the same results as baking in a regular oven. This oven bakes beautiful bread (two loaves at a time), rolls, muffins, casseroles, cookies and cakes. The foil in the box does not blacken, making it possible to use this oven for a very long time.

Instructions for making:

Supplies Needed: 1 sturdy apple box (20 inches x 13 inches and 12½ inches high).
                                extra cardboard to fill any handle holes
                                1 78-inch length heavy duty foil
                                1 84-inch length heavy duty foil
                                metal repair tape(foil tape)*
                                Optional for a window: 1 plastic oven bag
                                                      double-sided clear tape
                                                      metal repair tape(foil tape)**
                                                      box cutter
                                                       butter knife

*Masking tape may substituted in sticking the foil to the box. It must always be hidden inside the box to keep it from igniting. Over time it will loose stickiness, and need to be replaced.
**Duct tape may be substituted in making the window. Over time it peels away and will need to be replaced.

Pre-preparation:
1. If there are any holes, including handle holes, in your apple box cut extra cardboard to fill holes snuggly and cover patch with tape on both sides.
2. If an oven window is desired, cut a horizontal oven window (approx. 9x4 inches) in one of the long sides, centered and 2½ inches from the closed bottom of the box.

Covering the box:
    This box will be entirely covered inside and out with foil and secured with tape. Any exposed box inside will burn; therefore it is important to overlap foil.
1. The 78-inch length of foil will cover the inside and outside ends of the box and the outside only of the bottom.
   - Lay this foil shiny-side down. Position the box lengthwise and bottom down, centered on the foil strip.
   - Fold one length of the foil up the end and inside the box. This end of the foil should fold onto the inside bottom about 4 inches. Smooth foil out and ease into corners, allowing the extra to go onto the sides.
   - Making sure the foil on the end just covered is snug, repeat the same procedure for the other end of the box.
   - Fold excess foil on the outside edges of the box onto the box sides and secure foil every 4 inches or so with tape, both inside and outside the box.
2. The 84-inch length of foil will cover the inner and outer sides and bottom of the box.
   - Lay foil, shiny-side down. Position and center the box across the foil, so the foil will cover the bare sides.
   - Begin on the side of the box without a window. Fold the very end of the foil strip over 1 inch. Fold this end over the side of the box and position it into the inside crease where the bottom and the side meet.
   - Making sure the foil on the side just covered is snug, pull the foil around the bottom and up the side (covering the window), down the inside (covering the window) and across the bottom. Tuck the extra foil underneath the first edge with the 1-inch fold so it goes up the side.
   - Secure foil every 4 inches or so with tape, inside and outside the box.
3. If making the window:
   - Feel carefully for the window location.
   - Using scissors, cut a horizontal slit in the middle of the window hole, stopping 2 inches from each side. At each end, make diagonal cuts to the corners.

- You now have double flaps of foil on all sides of the window. Using a butter knife, carefully ease the inside flaps through the window and down between the box and the outside foil.
- Fold the outside flaps through the window to the inside of the box and secure with tape.
- Cut extra bits of foil and fold over window corners so that no part of the box is exposed. These will need to be pinched into place to secure them.
- Using a plastic oven bag, cut a double layer rectangle ½ inch larger than the window on all sides. To prolong the life of the window, secure bag over the outside of the window opening with double-stick tape placed slightly to the outside of the window edges to hide it from the heat. Repeat with the second layer of plastic bag.
- Secure outside plastic bag edges with foil tape.

Baking with an Applebox Reflector Oven:

<u>Supplies needed</u>:   4 empty soda pop cans, filled part way with rocks (so they won't tip over)
10x16-inch cookie cooling rack
chimney charcoal starter*
1 length heavy duty foil, longer than oven box (used for ground foil)
charcoal briquets
long-handled tongs
newspaper
matches
1-inch high rock

<u>Baking Steps</u>:
1. Place a piece of foil, shiny side up, on level ground or cement (not on anything flammable).
2. Space pop cans on foil so as to support the cookie cooling rack.
3. Position cooling rack so that only the very corners are resting on the pop cans. Check to make sure the cans are not spaced too far apart to prevent the applebox from fitting over them.
4. You will regulate the temperature of your oven by the number of briquets you put in it. **One briquet = approx. 35° F. Example—for 350° F use 10 charcoals.** Count out desired number of charcoals into a chimney charcoal starter. (In very cold, wet or cold windy weather an additional charcoal or two may be needed.) Place charcoal starter on a piece of foil on level ground or cement (not on anything flammable). Place 2 pieces of wadded-up newspaper in the base of the chimney charcoal starter and light. Allow to stand 5 min. until top briquets have a white spot at least the size of a dime.
5. Using tongs, place hot briquets on foil, spreading them out evenly between the cans and across the middle. Place cooking cooling rack on top of the cans.

6. To pre-heat oven, place the applebox over coals and empty rack, resting one corner on a 1-inch rock. (This allows enough air in the box for the charcoal to stay lit.) Let stand for 5 min. Charcoal will become whiter as heat spreads.
7. Carefully lift applebox off coals taking care not to tilt and place it beside the ground foil. (This holds trapped heat in the box.)
8. Quickly place food, in desired baking pan, on suspended cooling rack and replace box over coals, resting one corner on the rock. (Food cooked on a cookie sheet should be placed in from the corners as food directly over the cans will not cook.)
9. Charcoal will burn for 35-40 minutes. When longer cooking times are required, additional hot charcoals can be added by slightly lifting the box and slipping them in with long tongs.
10. When food is done, remove applebox and serve.
11. Safely deal with the charcoal, dust off the ground foil and fold loosely. It can be used again and again.

Note: Use light colored cooking/baking sheets/pans so that baked foods do not get too dark on the bottom.

Hint: When setting up oven, face the window toward the sun. This allows you to check the foods visually to see that they are done.

Second Hint: Baking once a day using an applebox reflector oven at about 400° F, will use an average of 12-13 charcoals/day. One lb. charcoal = 17 Kingsford© charcoal briquets. To bake for 1 year store 16 (20-lbs.) bags. This allows for a few extra briquets for wet or cold weather. Store additional charcoal for Dutch oven cooking.

Third Hint: For baking in freezing temperatures, place a doubled piece of wool blanket or other material that insulates on top of the box to retain inside heat.

Applebox Oven positioned over cooling rack for baking.
One corner rests on 1-inch rock to allow enough air for charcoal to burn.

*A chimney charcoal starter allows you to ignite charcoal without charcoal starter fluid, using only newspaper. It is well worth the effort to look for one to purchase. The most efficient kinds have holes going up the sides. This allows plenty of air to be drawn up through the inside, causing the charcoal to ignite more rapidly. Charcoal rests a third of the way up the starter on a rack, which gives space for wadded up newspaper underneath. The newspaper is then lit to ignite the charcoal. Always place the starter on a piece of heavy duty foil to prevent permanent blackening of your lovely concrete driveway or patio–which we can attest Does Happen!
©2003 Probert, Harkness <u>Emergency Food in a Nutshell, 2nd Edition, Revised</u>

FUEL OVERVIEW

It is critical that you read the General Safety Guidelines for Indoor and Outdoor Cooking which are not charted here.

FUEL	INDOOR COOKING OPTIONS	OUTDOOR COOKING OPTIONS	SHELF LIFE	PLANNING FOR LONG TERM USE/STORAGE
Wood	*†Wood-burning Stove–one pot cooking *Open Fireplace–one pot cooking *Cookstove–one pot cooking and baking	Open Fires–one pot cooking Cooking with Coals–Dutch oven and †Pit cooking	A very, very long time if covered and kept dry	Large amount required Store hardwood (burns longer) Large storage space required Good for heating & cooking
Coal	*Coal-burning Stove–one pot cooking		Anthracite–Indefinite Bituminous–Many years if kept dry	Large amount required Large storage space required Good for heating and cooking
Propane	Converted Gas Range–one pot cooking and baking *Imitation Wood stove–one pot cooking	Portable Camp Stove (table-top or free-standing)–one pot and †"Haybox" cooking Gas Barbecues–one pot cooking and baking Propane-fueled Generator–use of home appliances	Indefinite	Legal limits on amounts you store Cylinders must always be stored outside Good for cooking, some heating possibilities
Charcoal	NEVER	Dutch Oven–one pot cooking and baking †Volcano/Pyramid stoves–one pot cooking and baking †Applebox Reflector Oven–baking	Indefinite if kept away from moisture	Large amount required Space efficient Use only for cooking outdoors Easy to estimate quantity needed
Kerosene	*Cooker/Heater–one pot cooking		1 year–ideal Up to 3 years for high quality 1K kerosene if stored out of sunlight	Legal limits on amounts you store Store in garage/shed if allowed Cooking/heating possibilities
Gasoline	NEVER	Gasoline-fueled Generator–use of home appliances	1 year if stored in cool place in tightly sealed container	Legal limits on amounts you store Never store indoors Generator uses HUGE amt. of fuel

*Need alternate outside cooking option for hot weather months.
†Fuel efficient. These options help you conserve your fuel.

© 2003 Probert, Harkness, <u>Emergency Food in a Nutshell</u>, 2nd Edition, Revised

APPENDIX E

KEEPING YOUR COOL IN AN EMERGENCY: FOOD SAFETY WITHOUT A REFRIGERATOR

Learning to live without a refrigerator should electricity fail will be a challenge. Having lived with such a luxury, it will be a temptation to take unsafe risks when preparing food or keeping leftovers. The possibility of food poisoning is high. Common symptoms of foodborne illness include diarrhea, abdominal cramps, fever, headache and vomiting. It is not worth taking risks in an emergency.

Foods are kept safely in a refrigerator at temperatures of 40° F or lower. It would be wise to acquire a good thermometer so that you can accurately test the temperature of your food storage conditions before you attempt to store food like you would in a fridge. The following ideas can help you make some safe decisions.

- Whenever outside temperatures fall to 40° F or below, perishable foods can be safely stored in a protective container outside.
- An easy way to avoid worrying about storage temperature, is to simply plan meals so there are no perishable leftovers. This is your safest option when outside temperatures are above 40° F.
- It is wise to store a few small jars of foods that require refrigeration after opening such as mayonnaise, salad dressing, etc. Store jars that contain the amount needed for a single use.
- In warmer temperatures, it is still possible to cool food, including milk, fruits, and vegetables. Foods prepared in sanitary conditions can be cooled for up to 2 hours before they should be eaten. This applies to salads or cold soups. Consider the following ideas:

    Evaporative Cooler

    This is made with a heavy cloth draped over all sides of any kind of framework with shelves. The top of the cloth should sit in a container of water and acts as a wick to keep the entire cover wet. Place cooler in a shady place where the wind can blow over it. The greater the evaporation, the lower the temperature. Once the cooler is in place, thoroughly wet the cloth to start cooling.

    You may want to have two cloth covers to allow you to change the cooler cover each week. The used one can be sanitized by washing it and leaving it in the sun to dry.

    Cooler in the Ground

    In a shady place, dig a hole deep enough for a well made box or camping cooler to be placed below ground level. Place food inside and cover with a dampened heavy cloth. Cloth is kept wet by placing one end of it in a container of water.

    Root Cellars

    See your local extension service for information.

SOURCES:

Basic Self-Reliance, 1989. Church of Jesus Christ of Latter-day Saints.
Dian Thomas, Roughing It Easy, 1974.
U.S. Department of Agriculture
U.S. Food and Drug Adminstration

APPENDIX F

SPROUTING AND GARDENING FOR FRESH FOOD STORAGE

SPROUTS

Sprouts are seeds (beans or grains) which have been allowed to germinate in a moist environment for one to five days. Sprouts increase in vitamin content as they grow, making them more nutritious than the seeds from which they came.

Just how nutritious are sprouts anyway?

Sprouts are not the miracle food they are often claimed to be. They do not contain more nutrients than other foods. They do however, contain B vitamins, small amounts of vitamin A, protein, and trace minerals. Many other foods are better sources for these nutrients.

Sprouts also contain some vitamin C. Mung bean sprouts have the highest vitamin C content - ½ cup sprouts contains 11.7% RDA for vitamin C. By themselves, you would have to consume 5 cups of mung bean sprouts/day in order to reach the RDA for vitamin C. This illustrates the advantage of including other foods that contain vitamin C in a food storage plan.

What are the advantages of sprouting seeds during an emergency?

Sprouts add variety and flavor to a diet and, in places where the climate is too cold to grow fresh vegetables during the winter, they can be a wonderfully fresh and crunchy substitute for much missed fresh vegetables and salads.

The vitamin C content in sprouts could prevent scurvy in an emergency if they were the only source of vitamin C. Keep in mind, to do this, a person must eat 2-3 cups/day.

What precautions should I take when sprouting seeds?

Since 1995, concerns have arisen from outbreaks of E. Coli and Salmonella traced to alfalfa sprouts. Seeds that have been contaminated either by field animals or during post-harvest storage or by animal manure used to fertilize fields appear to be the problem. It is important to only buy and store seeds that are food grade and intended for human consumption. Additionally, do not use garden seeds or farm seeds as they may have been treated with a fungicide or pesticide which would be dangerous to consume.

How do I sprout seeds?

The three basics to sprouting are: moisture, warmth, and room to grow.
1. Remove broken or cracked seeds and rinse them thoroughly.
2. Soak seeds 8-10 hours or overnight at room temperature in four times their volume of water. In cold weather, seeds may need to soak a few more hours. One cup of seeds will make 3-6 cups of sprouts.
3. Rinse seeds in lukewarm water and drain well.
4. Place seeds in a container that allows them to drain. Too much moisture will cause mold to grow. Use a commercial sprouter, a glass jar with a piece of netting or clean nylon tied over the top, or a rust-proof colander.
5. Place the container in a well lit place out of direct sunlight. Sprouts will be greener when left to sprout on a counter and paler in color when sprouted in a cupboard. Both are delicious. Seeds sprout best between 75-85° F. Keep them away from drafts and out of direct heat. In colder months, slightly warm rinsing water will speed sprouting.
6. Rinse seeds 3-4 times daily to keep them moist. If you will be away, you can cover them with a damp towel to keep them moist. Seeds will not sprout with too little moisture.

7. Allow time for seeds to sprout:

Wheat	1-2 days
Lentils, corn	2-3 days
All beans (including mung beans), barley	3-4 days
Alfalfa	3-5 days

8. Rinse sprouts with cold water and drain thoroughly. Use sprouts at once or wrap them loosely in a single layer of damp paper towels. Put them in a tightly sealed plastic bag and store 7-10 days in the fridge. Sprouts can be used as snacks or in salads, stir-fried dishes, casseroles or dough.

   ‣ To minimize the introduction of bacteria into sprouts, thoroughly wash and rinse all sprouting equipment; then sanitize in a solution of 1 teaspoon bleach per 1 quart warm (not boiling) water and allow to air dry.

   ‣ Some kinds of seeds grow fuzzy roots which can look like mildew. These roots are actually a part of the sprout and are no cause for worry. Occasionally, real mildew can appear which is an indication that seeds need to be watered less frequently and moved to a cooler area.

   ‣ Storing beans and grains in nitrogen packed (oxygen depleted) containers does not affect their ability to sprout. Seeds less than 5 years old have the best capacity to sprout. Seeds sprout best when they have been stored in a dark place at cool temperatures and in low humidity.

SOURCES:

> Suzanne Clegg and Beth K. Thorson, USU Foods/Nutrition Specialists
> FDA Consumer
> Kitchen Crop Sprouter, NK Lawn & Garden Company
> University of Idaho, Cooperative Extension System
> U.S. Department of Agriculture
> Utah State University Extension Service

GARDENING

Nothing compares to the taste and nutrition of fresh fruits and vegetables. You will be very grateful to have a source of fresh foods during a prolonged difficulty. It is critical to prepare now. Growing a garden takes some practice and will require supplies that may not be readily available in an emergency.

How do I garden—I don't have any space?

Don't worry if you don't have a traditional garden plot, many foods can be grown in small places with some creativity. A variety of vegetables and herbs, and even strawberries can be grown in pots on a balcony, porch or sunny window. These can also be used as borders in a typical flower garden. The important thing is that you start now to try to grow a few things.

It is possible to find a vacant lot or space where, with permission of the owner, a garden could be planted. Several families could go together to farm a lot. Work could also be exchanged for produce when someone needs assistance with their garden. If you have your own yard, consider planning a garden plot and planting a fruit tree or two.

How do I store seeds?

Seeds purchased in one season can be stored until the next growing season if stored in a sealed container (canning jar with secured lid, plastic container with snap-on lid, or sealed plastic bag) to keep away from moisture and air. A little dry milk may be placed in the container to absorb moisture. Additionally, the container must be kept in a cool, dark location. Seeds may be left in their original packages in the above storage conditions. This makes it possible to have an inexpensive year's supply, tailored to your taste, on hand at all times. Seeds stored over a year may not germinate.

Seeds can also be purchased in nitrogen packaged #10 cans. These seeds may be stored up to five years with successful germination.

Of course, you can always learn to harvest and save your own seeds from the plants you grow in your garden. However, you will not be able to successfully grow the same plants from seeds of hybrid varieties.

How can I get the most from my garden to help with my food storage?

When space is limited, plant fruits and vegetables that give the most yield for the space they require. For example, corn and peas use a great deal of space for a small yield. Beets, carrots, green beans and squash produce greater quantities for the space they occupy. Besides the usual bean and cucumber, other vining plants such as squash and cantaloupe can be grown vertically. Your local extension service will have information on growing two or three crops in the same garden area e.g., squash at the base of corn.

A garden harvest can be completely wiped out by an unsuspected soil virus brought on by planting the same crops in the same places year after year. Contact your local extension service for information on how to prevent such soil diseases. They will also have a wealth of other gardening information applicable to your climate.

To make the results of your garden last through the winter months, produce can be bottled and dried, or you can explore cold storage possibilities. Look for information on these and other techniques for preserving food at your local extension service.

Ideas for battling weeds?

There are many ideas and practices that are helpful. A super easy solution is to buy a black ground cloth, which prevents weeds from growing while allowing water to penetrate into the soil. Simply cut holes in cloth and plant desired seeds or seedlings.

SOURCES:

Thanks to Apryl Cox for some great ideas!

Appendix G

Do-It-Yourself Packaging for Long Term Storage

The very best and easiest way to ensure the long-term safety of your food is to buy it already sealed in airtight containers. This not only assures you of the absence of insects, but also preserves nutrition in optimum storage conditions. When this is not feasible, one of the following methods can be used to protect stored food. Keep in mind, in the presence of oxygen, the long- term shelf life of foods will decrease.

In most kinds of food that come in non-airtight packaging, there is the possibility of an insect or insect egg. Always open the package and carefully check for insects on the top of the product. If none are found, you may choose to pour product into five to six gallon plastic buckets, seal with lids, and wait two to three weeks (incubation time for any insect eggs). Inspect product for insects; they will crawl to the top. If no insects are found, it is probably not infested with insect eggs. Inspect product again one week later to be sure. If any insects are found at any time, the DRY ICE or FREEZING methods will be necessary to safely store food. Otherwise, product can be stored in a container only.

Containers should be food grade with tight-fitting lids to protect contents from moisture and rodents.

Dry Ice Method

Dry ice evaporates, producing fumes of $CO2$ which are heavier than air and replace the oxygen in the container.

In humid environments moisture in the air can condense on dry ice and introduce water into the storage container increasing the risk of mold growth. For this reason, the dry ice method is only recommended for use in dry climates.

Begin by placing two to three inches of product in bottom of container (usually five to six gallon plastic food grade bucket). Put two ounces of crushed dry ice on top, and fill the rest of bucket with product. Place the lid loosely on the bucket—do not seal it. The dry ice will release carbon dioxide which replaces oxygen in the container. Wait approximately 30 minutes to two hours for ice to vaporize, then seal lid. Feel the bottom of the bucket, if icy-cool there is still dry ice present. Over the next hour, check the bucket frequently for bulging which indicates the dry ice has not completely vaporized. If bucket bulges, carefully loosen the lid for a few minutes and then reseal it.

This method will kill any adult or larval insects present, but may not destroy the eggs or pupae. To kill the latter, it may be necessary to repeat this process after two to three weeks. Check your product for insects before doing again. If product is able to be sealed in an airtight container after the first fumigation, a second is not necessary.

Freezing

Freezing will usually kill insects if the temperature is cold enough. One to ten lbs. of product can be put in plastic freezer bags and frozen in a deep freeze for two to three days. To check if your freezer is cold enough, spread contents of a bag on a cookie and let thaw to room temperature. Check for live insects. If found, repeat freezing process. Product can then be emptied into a well-sealed, rodent-proof container. It is not necessary that the container be airtight. After three weeks, open container and check for live insects; insects will crawl to top. If insects are found, repeat freezing process.

Oxy Pack in Sealed Containers

This involves placing product and an oxygen absorber packet in a container that can be sealed so it is airtight (a #10 can, mylar bag, or five to six gallon bucket). This method has the advantage of sealing foods in an oxygen depleted environment which preserves nutrition and shelf life.

A few suppliers sell sealers and mylar bags or canners and #10 cans along with oxy absorber packs. These can be used to store low-moisture foods for a long time. The cost of these sealers or canners can be offset when a large group shares the cost. Bags, cans, and oxy absorber packs are usually less expensive when bought in bulk for a group of people.

SOURCES:
University of Utah Extension Services

152

APPENDIX H

LIST OF SUPPLIERS

We have had personal interaction with the following companies which ship their products all over the U.S. Check the Internet and consult your local churches and community groups for further resources. Form your own neighborhood co-op for larger buying power, greater discounts, and faster delivery.

Country Store and Kitchen Specialties
9336 NE 76th St Vancouver, WA 98662
(360) 256-9131 Orders (888) 311-8940 FAX (360) 687-0939
www.healthyharvest.com E-Mail countrystore@healthyharvest.com
Offers wide variety of grains, legumes, flours and mixes, dried fruits and vegetables, pastas, soup bases and drink mixes, dried dairy and egg products, cooking aids, herbs and spices, emergency preparedness items and first aid kits. Can buy items in nitrogen packed #10 cans or buckets and also in bulk. (Bulk quantities are not always packaged for long-term storage.) Request catalog.

Emergency Essentials
216 E. University Parkway Orem, Utah 84058-7601
(801) 222-9667
www.beprepared.com E-Mail at webmaster@beprepared.com
Offers wide variety of grains, legumes, flours and mixes, dried fruits and vegetables, pastas, soup bases and drink mixes, dried dairy and egg products, and cooking aids all nitrogen packed in #10 cans or buckets. Also carries MRE's and many preparedness items. Discounted group specials. Request catalog.

Grandma's Country Foods
386 W. 9400 S. Sandy, Ut 84070
(801)748-0808 FAX (801)572-8960
www.grandmascountry.com
Offers variety of spices, freeze-dried and dried foods, as well as dried milk and calcium-fortified soy milk. Can buy items in nitrogen packed #10 cans and buckets and also in bulk.

Honeyville Grain Company
635 N. Billy Mitchell Drive Salt Lake City Utah 84116
(801) 972-2168 FAX (801) 972-8412
Offers large variety of grains, flours, legume and soy products, cooking aids, some mixes. Items are not packaged for long term-storage. Call for catalog.

Nitro-Pak Preparedness Center
475 W. 910 S. Heber City, Utah 84032
(435) 657-4100 Orders (800) 866-4876 or FAX (888) 648-7672
www.nitro-pak.com
Offers wide variety of grains, legumes, flours and mixes, dried fruits and vegetables, pastas, soup bases and drink mixes, dried dairy and egg products and cooking aids all nitrogen packed in #10 cans or buckets. Large distributor of freeze-dried foods. Also carries many emergency preparedness items. Request catalog.

Provident Living Center
Jeannie Sorensen 729 W. 350 S. Orem, Ut 84058
(801)226-0635 OR (800)723-0635
www.providentlivingcenter.com
      Offers wide variety of grains, legumes, flours and mixes, dried fruits and vegetables, pastas, soup bases and drink mixes, dried dairy and egg products, cooking aids, herbs and spices, and emergency preparedness items at great prices. Can buy items in nitrogen packed #10 cans or buckets and also in bulk. Ships anywhere.

San Francisco Herb Company
250 14th St. San Francisco, CA 94103-2495
(415) 861-7174
www.sfherb.com
      Great source for fresh herbs and spices and some dehydrated vegetables. Items are not packaged for long-term storage. Minimum order. Call for catalog.

Walton Feed, Inc.
135 N. 10th P.O. Box 307 Montpelier, Idaho 83254
(208) 847-0465   (800) 847-0465   FAX (208) 847-0467
www.waltonfeed.com
      Offers large variety of grains, legumes, flours and mixes, dried fruits and vegetables, pastas, soup bases and drink mixes, dried dairy and egg products, cooking aids, herbs and spices, emergency preparedness items and first aid kits. Can buy items in nitrogen packed #10 cans or buckets and also in bulk. (Bulk quantities are not always packaged for long-term storage.) Request catalog.

Note: If ham bouillon is not available in your area, check the Internet for suppliers.

154

Appendix I

What Can I Make With. . . .?: Index by Ingredient

One of the first questions a person asks as he or she begins to store food is, "If I buy _____ how am I going to use it?" This appendix indexes specific ingredients to recipes in this book. The index does not include baking powder or soda, salt, white sugar, spices, or flavorings which are commonly used in a great number of recipes.

Should you find that a food you store is reaching the end of its shelf life, this index gives you recipes to help you use it.

164

Vegetables, canned/bottled (cont.)
    potato, slices
        Country Meat Pie, 89
    pumpkin
        Impossible Pumpkin Pie, 101
        Pumpkin Cookies, 111
        Pumpkin Squares, 111
    spaghetti sauce
        Bean or Beef Spaghetti, 85
        Lasagne, 87
    tomato paste
        Barbecue Beef Casserole, 90
        Minestrone, 70
        Spicy Hungarian Lentil Stew, 75
        White Bean and Turkey Chili, 74
    tomato sauce
        8 Bean Soup, 69
        Beef or Chicken and Bean Enchiladas, 86
        Cheesy Beans and Rice, 81
        Fantastic French Dressing, 67
        Seven Layer Chicken Casserole, 93
        Southwestern Chicken or Turkey
            Barley Soup, 77
        Spanish Rice, 98
        Stretch-A-Can of Baked Beans, 83
        Sweet & Sour Beef, 91
    tomatoes, diced
        Barbecue Beef Casserole, 90
        Bean and Bacon Hot Pot, 75
        Beef Goulash, 91
        Buckaroo Beans, 72
        Chili on Spaghetti, 86
        Curry Beef on Rice, 91
        Eureka Kidney Bean Soup, 71
        Fabulous Soup Mix Soup, 69
        Ham 'N Bean Soup, 73
        Lentil Bacon Soup, 75
        Lentil Chili, 71
        Lentil Stew, 71
        Lentil Vegetable Soup, 72
        Mexican Bean Sauce with Fettuccine, 81
        Quick Beef Chili and Corn, 73
        Southwestern Chicken or Turkey
            Barley Soup, 77
        Split Pea Stew, 72
        Swiss Steak and Parsley Potato Rounds, 90
        Tomato Risotto, 98
        Tomatoes-on-the-side, 98
    tomatoes, stewed
        Mexican Bean Sauce with Fettuccine, 81
        Vegetarian Chili, 71
    yellow beans
        Five Bean Salad, 66

Vegetables, dried
    any vegetable
        Reckless Ramen, 78
        Simply Delicious Beans, 70
    broccoli
        Broccoli Soup, 69
        Chicken Broccoli Twist, 93
        Creamy Broccoli and Tuna, 95
        Creamy Broccoli Rice Soup, 68
        Vegetable Cheese Soup, 68
    cabbage
        Any Bean Soup with Vegetables, 70
        Minestrone, 70
    carrots
        8 Bean Soup, 69
        Any Bean Soup with Vegetables, 70
        Beef Barley Stew, 76
        Beef Stew, 76
        Chicken Broccoli Twist, 93
        Chicken Corn Soup, 77
        Chicken 'N Dumplings, 78
        Complete-meal Tuna Helper, 95
        Country Meat Pie, 89
        Creamy Chicken and Rice Soup, 77
        Creamy Red Beans and Pasta Salad, 62
        Fried Rice, 80
        Lentil Bacon Soup, 75
        Lentil Stew, 71
        Lentil Vegetable Soup, 72
        Lima Bean Soup, 74
        Minestrone, 70
        Split Pea Soup, 76
        Split Pea Stew, 72
        Sweet & Sour Beef, 91
        Swiss Steak and Parsley Potato Rounds, 90
        Vegetable Cheese Soup, 68
    celery
        8 Bean Soup, 69
        Any Bean Soup with Vegetables, 70
        Bean and Bacon Hot Pot, 75
        Beef Barley Stew, 76
        Chicken Corn Soup, 77
        Chicken 'N Dumplings, 78
        Chicken Noodle Salad, 64
        Creamy Chicken and Rice Soup, 77
        Curry Beef on Rice, 91
        Lentil Bacon Soup, 75
        Lentil Vegetable Soup, 72
        Minestrone, 70
        New England Clam Chowder, 79
        Potato Soup, 68
        Senate Bean Soup, 73
        Spam and Pasta Salad, 64
        Split Pea Stew, 72
        Tropical Chicken Salad, 65
        Tuna Noodle Salad, 65

APPENDIX J

The primary focus of this book is on storing food for an emergency and how to cook with it. There are also non-food necessities you will want to have on hand that we do not address herein. The scope of these items and their quantities will depend on your personal preferences and needs, geographic location, and budget. The following charts are provided for you to plan for these non-food needs. They are included here so they can be conveniently kept with your food storage plan.

NON-FOOD STORAGE ITEMS Use the following space to plan for items such as personal hygiene supplies, first-aid supplies, clothing, blankets, sewing supplies, cleaning supplies, fuel, and cooking equipment.			
ITEM	Total Quantity Needed	Amount on Hand	Quantity to Buy

NON-FOOD STORAGE ITEMS (CONT.)			
ITEM	Total Quantity Needed	Amount on Hand	Quantity to Buy

NON-FOOD STORAGE ITEMS (CONT.)			
ITEM	Total Quantity Needed	Amount on Hand	Quantity to Buy

NON-FOOD STORAGE ITEMS (CONT.)			
ITEM	Total Quantity Needed	Amount on Hand	Quantity to Buy

INDEX

ABOUT THE AUTHORS

Leslie Probert: Bachelor of Science degree in Home Economics, mother of three, married to Australian husband and lived in Australia 13 years. Brave and supportive husband had never tasted a dried bean recipe in his life before this book. Family rejoiced when we found enough good tasting bean recipes so we could quit experimenting! The cinnamon roll experiments were the best!

Lisa Harkness: Bachelor of Science degree in Political Science, mother of five, married to unusually comical and cooperative American husband. Children were glad when mom worked with Leslie on this book because she gave them many extra treats to divert them while she wrote. Sadly, for them, and finally, for her, this is finished.